®
teach
yourself

basic website creation

peter cope

Launched in 1938, the **teach yourself** series grew rapidly in response to the world's wartime needs. Loved and trusted by over 50 million readers, the series has continued to respond to society's changing interests and passions and now, 70 years on, includes over 500 titles, from Arabic and Beekeeping to Yoga and Zulu. What would you like to learn?

Be where you want to be with **teach yourself**

For UK order enquiries: please contact Bookpoint Ltd, 130 Milton Park, Abingdon, Oxon OX14 4SB. Telephone: +44 (0)1235 827720. Fax: +44 (0)1235 400454. Lines are open 09.00–17.00, Monday to Saturday, with a 24-hour message answering service. Details about our titles and how to order are available at www.teachyourself.co.uk.

For USA order enquiries: please contact McGraw-Hill Customer Services, PO Box 545, Blacklick, OH 43004-0545, USA. Telephone: 1-800-722-4726. Fax: 1-614-755-5645.

For Canada order enquiries: please contact McGraw-Hill Ryerson Ltd, 300 Water St, Whitby, Ontario L1N 9B6, Canada. Telephone: 905 430 5000. Fax: 905 430 5020.

Long renowned as the authoritative source for self-guided learning – with more than 50 million copies sold worldwide – the **teach yourself** series includes over 500 titles in the fields of languages, crafts, hobbies, business, computing and education.

British Library Cataloguing in Publication Data: a catalogue record for this title is available from The British Library.

Library of Congress Catalog Card Number: on file.

First published in UK 2008 by Hodder Education, part of Hachette Livre UK, 338 Euston Road, London NW1 3BH.

First published in USA 2008 by The McGraw-Hill Companies Inc.

The **teach yourself** name is a registered trademark of Hodder Headline.

Computer hardware and software brand names mentioned in this book are protected by their respective trademarks and are acknowledged.

The publisher has used its best endeavours to ensure that the URLs for external websites referred to in this book are correct and active at the time of going to press. However, the publisher has no responsibility for the websites and can give no guarantee that a site will remain live or that the content is or will remain appropriate.

Typeset by Mac Bride, Southampton

Printed in Great Britain for Hodder Education, an Hachette Livre UK Company, 338 Euston Road, London NW1 3BH, by CPI Cox & Wyman, Reading, Berkshire RG1 8EX.

Hachette Livre UK's policy is to use papers that are natural, renewable and recyclable products and made from wood grown in sustainable forests. The logging and manufacturing processes are expected to conform to the environmental regulations of the country of origin.

Impression number   10 9 8 7 6 5 4 3 2 1

Year   2011 2010 2009 2008

contents

preface

Watch a television programme, read a newspaper item or scan advertisements and chances are you'll almost expect to see a website address where you can go to find out more. Suddenly, it seems everyone and every organization, club and company is on the Web. No subject is too pedestrian to justify a website. It's a safe supposition that in reading this book you're considering adding to their number and variety by creating you own.

The good news is that in doing so now you're probably better placed than ever for getting a good presence on the Web. Why? Because creating a website has never been easier. There are some good reasons for this.

First, the Internet has changed and continues to change in scope. It's been adopted across the world and across all classes of society. You are just as likely to find resources and web pages designed for senior citizens as you are teenagers (in fact, in some areas, more likely) and pages of lightweight gossip are just as likely as academic treatises. To accommodate all these new users, all elements of the Web need to be easy to use. Hence you can benefit from this ease of use.

Second, all the technology that underpins the Internet – from the computers used to create websites and those used to view them through the broadband connections that link the essential components to the vast servers where websites are stored – is much more potent. While older websites might have been text-only, today's are just as likely to feature photos, movies and music.

Third, and perhaps most significantly for the purposes of this book, the software used for website creation is now widely available, absurdly simple to use and makes no presumptions on the user's computer skills. No longer do you need to be an expert in programming to produce the most elementary of web pages; anyone today can, with just a little practice, produce the slickest and most compelling of web pages. You really can be up and running on the World Wide Web in minutes.

With contemporary software applications you can, far more easily, create a site that has visual impact, attracts visitors (and visitors that will return on more than one occasion) and could even earn you money.

So, how do you achieve your ambition of creating a popular and well-regarded website? The process is best described by breaking it down into logical chunks, each of which will be addressed through this book:

1 **Planning:** resist the temptation to go straight to your computer and start creating your first web page. Do you want a conventional website or would your ambitions be better satisfied by an online journal – a blog – or a photo gallery? Careful analysis at this stage will save a great deal of time and effort later.

2 **Design and style:** achieving a website that stands out from the crowd (for all the best reasons) requires that you spend a little time designing the site. A coherent, well-designed site will always win over a more prosaic design or one with a more haphazard collection of design elements.

3 **Produce content:** a website, no matter how attractive or slick is really only a vehicle to deliver content. That content may be text-based information, a collection of images, music or even video. Or it may comprise all these media types. It's important that this content is collected in preparation for use on the site.

4 **Site authoring:** you can now use your chosen web authoring applications (these too will be discussed in detail later) to build your site. Thanks to modern software you'll be pleased to hear that this is one of the easier tasks, even more so if your chosen format of website is a blog or a photo gallery.

5 **Testing:** Once you've completed your basic website you need to test it to ensure that visitors and surfers will get the experience on the site that you anticipated. You'll need to check that any links you've built in work and that the look of the website is preserved when you use different web browsers.

6 **Promoting your site:** your site will compete with many others for visitors, so it'll be important to advertise and promote your site. This will ensure that you get the right exposure in search engines (such as the ubiquitous Google) and have links to your site from those of your peers.

Assumptions and conventions

I will assume that you have some familiarity with visiting websites – but no more. I shall explain the key terminology of the Web – and of websites in particular.

As for computer use and familiarity, I'll assume you've an everyday knowledge: sufficient, say, to use a word processor (or Microsoft Office, for example), send e-mails and to download images from a digital camera.

I have also aimed to keep jargon to an absolute minimum but, as you might expect, it's impossible to remove all jargon when discussing websites, web pages, the Internet and computers. To make up for this I have included an extensive glossary at the end of this book so that you can quickly gain an insight into any terms that may have been mentioned in passing and that you are not familiar with.

Just a final word on computer platforms. The Internet is pretty much egalitarian with respect to the computers attached to it. Hence, whether you choose to use a Windows PC, a Macintosh computer or even a Linux model, the approach and techniques for website creation are the same. I've pointed out differences where they are relevant.

Website or web site? There seems no logical rule on this so I've tended to follow the herd and talk about web pages and websites. And the Internet and the Web are capitalized, by convention.

So, let us start upon the adventure of creating websites and gaining that presence on the World Wide Web!

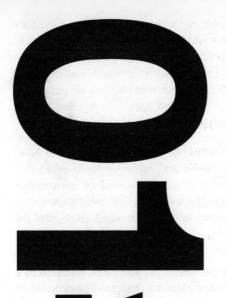

01

websites and how they work

In this chapter you will learn:

- about the background of the Internet
- some of the key terminology
- about browsers

Introduction

Around a quarter of the world's six and a half billion people use the Internet. Some use it for fun, some for business and many for both. A child of the Cold War, the Internet today is all-pervasive. It delivers e-mail, information – even television programming – at the touch of that proverbial button. And, whilst it was once the preserve of computer users with computers physically linked to a telephone line, the Internet is now easily accessible from wireless laptops, mobile phones and other portable devices. It has taken over from libraries as the key source of information even if, by virtue of its egalitarian nature, that information may not always be strictly correct or as precise as that offered by print media.

The Internet has given everyone the opportunity to have a voice that can be heard around the world. As such it is, potentially, a fantastic gift. However, since everyone has the opportunity to have a presence on the Internet, any individual keen to say something important or wanting to get noticed will need not only to produce a website that deserves to be seen but ensure that potential visitors have every opportunity to find it.

Evolution of the Internet

Neither of these tasks is particularly onerous but before we discover why, let's begin by taking a look at how the Internet has evolved into the – mostly tame – beast that it is today. You will then see how the key technologies, those technologies that will be central to our website design and promotion, arose.

Like so many fundamental technologies, the Internet was born of military need. In the years immediately after the Second World War, as the Cold War entered its early phases, the importance of robust communication between military units was being recognized. Strategists emphasized the need for it but, with their technical advisers, pointed to the vulnerability of communications to attack and particularly nuclear attack.

These advisers pointed out an essential problem with the telephone communications systems of the day. A telephone system was comprised of groups of telephone lines routed through a central exchange. At this exchange incoming phone calls could be routed or directed to another phone line connected to that exchange or to another and, then, onward to a line connected to that. No matter how robust the individual components, an attack that took out a central telephone exchange would render all connected phone lines useless.

The solution was a system that had redundancy: multiple stages and routes that could, if one were to fail (or be knocked out by military action) continue operating by merely redirecting calls on an alternative route. So, rather than having a telephone that connected through that single, vulnerable exchange, computers would talk to each other directly (or indirectly) over a 'network'. When one computer wanted to talk to another (or, rather, the user of one computer wanted to talk to the user of another) the message would be converted to digital data and this data would travel in small chunks (known as packets) that would navigate around the network using the most convenient route until arriving at the destination. Should any branch of this network be compromised then the packets would continue to travel around using any of the alternative routes.

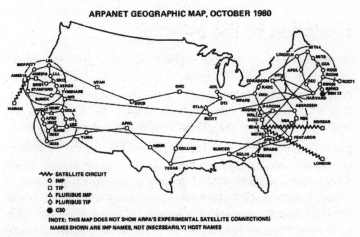

Figure 1.1 ARPAnet showing the interlinked network of military sites

This embryonic network – dubbed ARPAnet – was modest in its scope and reach but did lay down some firm foundations. Within just a few years it had grown to be a global network of computers not just limited to military use: ARPAnet had become the Internet.

The Internet and the World Wide Web

Despite being increasingly popular, the Internet was still a tool that could only be seriously exploited by those who were sufficiently adept at managing its complex technical core and countless idiosyncrasies. It was certainly not something that could ever be described as suitable for – and usable by – the rest of us.

Birth of the Web

That would take the creation of the World Wide Web. Also known by its initials, WWW or simply called the Web, this was the advance that would help move the Internet into the mainstream. We have the British physicist Tim Berners-Lee to thank for its creation. Like many great inventions and discoveries, his idea was remarkably simple but also remarkably powerful. Berners-Lee used the concept of hypertext – electronic text that is interlinked with other information – as a key resource on the Internet. This is a powerful cross-referencing and linking system that made it simple to link to documents wherever they resided on the Internet. A file on a computer on the other side of the world is as accessible as one in a neighbouring room.

Despite being originally designed for the sharing of academic papers between physicists and institutions, the concept proved equally suitable (and equally easy to invoke) for any documents. Discrete documents could now become interlinked web pages.

It's probably worth clarifying and emphasizing the terms 'Internet' and 'World Wide Web' as the two terms often get used (even by those that should know better) interchangeably. The Internet is the worldwide network of computers connected to each other by wire or wireless links. The World Wide Web is one application of the Internet. You can use the Internet for other purposes too, including e-mailing, instant messaging and bulletin boards. I will do my best not to confuse the two in this book!

The Language of the Web

Tim Berners-Lee's fundamental contribution to the Internet was based on the use of a special Internet language called Hypertext Markup Language or HTML. Though it looks rather like conventional computer programming language, HTML (which is still in use today) is actually a set of instructions that describes how a web page should look. Everything from the placement of text on the web page through to the colour and size of that text, the inclusion and positioning of additional media and the hyperlinks to other pages is defined by the HTML for that page.

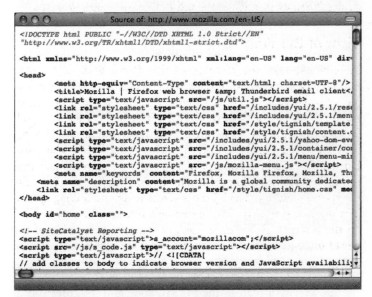

Figure 1.2 Rather abstract when first seen, HTML is actually a set of instructions on how to display information. This HTML is an excerpt from that used to display the screen in Figure 1.3

HTML is a pretty straightforward language to use – given just a modest amount of experience – but is not the most intuitive way to construct a web page. Fortunately the days when it was a requirement to use HTML to build a web page are long gone. Today, you'll be pleased to hear, you can construct web pages using tools that are the Web equivalent of desktop publishing applications. You can type text onto a page in the size, font and colour that you require. You can add images and place them where you wish. You can even mark those parts of the page you want to link – hyperlink – to other pages or websites. When you are done, the essential HTML code that interprets your layout for the computer (and the Web) is automatically generated.

Does that mean that a knowledge of HTML programming is now redundant? No, not quite. It can still be useful to have a basic knowledge of HTML to get the best from website creation and there will still be a few techniques that HTML can do that you won't be able to do with some web page creation software. That's why many website design professionals use only HTML and more recent variants and developments of the language. Programming in HTML often helps produce more compact websites that are more efficiently downloaded – crucial for some commercial sites.

Surfing the Web: the web browser

Before we get down to creating web pages and websites I will spend a moment examining the way that websites are viewed. Whether you surf the Web using your computer or a hand-held device – such as a personal digital assistant (PDA) or mobile phone – you'll generally explore web pages using a special computer program called a web browser.

More often just called a 'browser' these are special applications designed to display websites and pages. Essentially they are interpreters: when you direct the browser to look at a web page the browser will read in the HTML code and interpret this as the corresponding web page.

You'll probably find that your computer comes with a browser pre-installed. That tends to be Internet Explorer if you are using a Windows PC and Safari (**www.apple.com/safari**) if you are using a Macintosh computer. Although these are the preferred browsers from the respective manufacturers, you are not obliged to use them. You can download – easily and freely – alternatives. Firefox (**www.mozilla.com/firefox**) is a popular option for both Windows PCs and Macintosh computers, and Safari (which is the default browser on iPhones) is also available for Windows

PCs. At the time of writing, Google had just launched its Chrome browser for Windows PCs and Macintosh computers. To put things in perspective, here's an example of the relative shares of the market for web browsers in the first half of 2008:

- Internet Explorer: 74%
- Firefox: 18%
- Safari: 6%
- Opera: 0.7%
- Netscape: 0.6%

Are all browsers the same? Yes and no. Yes, all browsers perform the same role (of representing HTML instructions) but no, they don't necessarily do so in exactly the same way. That means that a website or web page that displays in one way using, say, Internet Explorer may not look precisely the same with Safari. That can be down to the inherent design of a particular browser or the setting made in that browser's preferences. These allow you to configure certain parameters of the web page display –

Figure 1.3 Firefox 3 web browser

for example changing the size (or colour) that text is displayed: crucial if the user has sight problems for example.

Although it's often hard to predict any changes that browsers apply to a web page it is important that, once you've constructed your website, you check the appearance using different ones. There will be rare occasions when your carefully crafted site will behave unpredictably with different browsers.

Note that browsers can also be used to display files and documents stored locally on your own computer. Often software application manufacturers will create their documentation in a form that can be used through a browser. This allows seamless integration with the Internet (for access to additional resources) and takes advantage of the tools offered by the browser (such as the forward/backward buttons and searching facilities) to help users navigate.

I will make the presumption at this point that you are reasonably familiar with browsers. Sufficiently familiar to find a website, use the forward and backward buttons to move through selected pages and, perhaps save favourite pages as Favorites or bookmarks. Any additional skills that might be required will be discussed later.

Summary

This chapter should have given you a good understanding of where the Internet came from and how its fundamental modes of operation arose. You should also now be aware of HTML, used for creating web pages even if, in creating your own pages, you never actually use it.

Ahead of the next chapter, where you will begin to get to grips with the elements that comprise web pages and the different websites' formats, you might want to use the links given on page 6 to download alternative browsers and get familiar with their slightly different features. You'll need to use these later to test out your website.

02 essentials of website creation

In this chapter you will learn:

- about different types of websites
- about their essential components
- how the different elements can be most effectively used
- how web pages can be linked to create a website

The Web is awash with websites and web pages, each of which seems at first glance to be unique. In fact when you study a little more closely you'll see that websites tend to conform to one of a small range of formats. Likewise web pages, although differing in layout and content, will share a high degree of commonality in the key components. Some layouts work better than others and web designers tend to focus on best practice.

In this chapter you will discover those components of a web page that will form the basis of your pages, along with the ways in which these pages can be linked together to form a website. I will begin by taking an overview of the different types of website that you might want to create.

Website types

Given a knowledge of web technologies – such as HTML – the adept programmer can, from first principles, create any type of website. The secret, as they say, is in the coding. You or I, without that extensive knowledge, can resort to templates and pre-configured designs to create almost as broad a range of sites. Let's look at the main types of website you are likely to encounter and, perhaps, want to emulate.

Blogs

Weblogs – or blogs for short – are online diaries that tell visitors about the person or their activities in chronological order. These sites are simple to set up and, to those versed in using social networking sites such as Facebook or Bebo, the construction will be very familiar. Though you could create a blog from scratch, generally, all you need to do to get one up and running and accessible across the Web, is to create an account with a blogging site, give your blog a name and choose a layout. After that, the content is down to you. That content is normally text-based but most blogging sites allow you to add images whilst some also allow you to enliven your blog with movie clips and other multimedia resources.

Despite this simplicity some very popular websites are based on simple blogs and for getting a web presence fast they are hard to

Figure 2.1 A blog is a website that usually features the creator's journal

beat. You can also, as your familiarity with the design of websites increases, append your blog to another website.

Photo albums

There's no doubt that digital photography has re-invigorated the medium of photography and caused the number of photos shot every year (once in strong decline) to skyrocket. For many, the beauty of digital photography is the immediacy and the opportunity to share photos quickly with friends and family around the world. Creating a photo-album website allows you to share whole albums of images with anyone you care to give the website address to.

Creating an online photo album is simple and you can do so via many of the photo printing and sharing websites. If you prefer to go solo you can also use the tools provided in many photo editing and retouching applications (such as Adobe Photoshop and Photoshop Elements) to produce your own web-ready gallery. This option requires a little more work as you'll need to post your completed work to a website. Don't worry, though, as we'll cover all the mechanics of this in the following chapters.

General websites

If your web ambitions are neither catered for by weblogs or photo albums you'll need to create your own website. Again you can do this using some simple templates (assuming those templates cater for the look you require) and even use simple applications such as Microsoft Office. At the top end you can use powerful website creation software, software that we take a closer look at in the next chapter.

Collaborative websites and wikis

If you are creating a website that requires the input of a number of people you've a range of options. You could act as the senior point of contact, the webmaster, for the site. Everyone wanting to put content on the site would need to contact you with the information they wish to post and you would have the perhaps-onerous task of adding all that information.

If the amount of information to be added was modest that might not be a problem, but for larger amounts, or for information that might be particularly complex, you might want others to contribute directly. This is how wiki sites and, in particular Wikipedia, rely on growing. The site features tools that users who register can use to add brand-new content or modify existing content. On a major site such as Wikipedia different levels of safeguards are also put in place to stop potentially malevolent visitors damaging that data already entered for their own mischievous purposes.

For other websites, software exists (such as Adobe/Macromedia Contribute) that allows multiple users in different locations access to the content of a website and allows them to perform modifications.

Anatomy of web pages

To a greater or lesser degree we are all familiar with the look of websites. Before going any further it is important that you are also familiar with the components that go together to form those websites and will, ultimately help you build your own websites and web pages.

There's something of an urge in us all to bypass the manuals and instruction books that come with any hardware or software we may buy. Rather than spend time reading we want to get straight down to business. So, if you are inclined to skip this chapter, make sure you bookmark it, as it will be one that you'll need to visit – and revisit – as your constructional work progresses.

Though few of us are architects, it's useful to draw an analogy in website construction with house building. If you were to set out to build a house from scratch you would begin by planning. You would consider the components: the doors, walls, floors and windows. And you would, perhaps before considering the layout, calculate the amount of space that you would need. How the components are arranged to make best use of the space, and how those components are arranged are crucial to a successful project. So it is with website building.

Because there is no absolute 'right' and 'wrong' in website design it is important to recognize that the way you put together the elements described here is not prescribed; how you do so is down to your own style, something we take a closer look at in the next chapters.

Let's take a look now at the key components – some obvious, some less so – common to all websites.

Home pages

When you first arrive at a website you'll generally, unless you have used a search engine (such as Google) to find a specific page, arrive at the site's home page. This is where you'll find (or should find, if the site has been properly constructed) all the essential information that a visitor to the site should need. And from here you will also be able to navigate (that is, move to) to

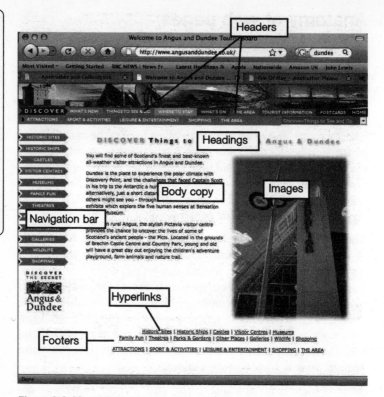

Figure 2.2 Many of the features of a web page are common to all – or most – websites. Here are the features you'll discover in this chapter

other parts of the site. Think of it as the equivalent of the front page of a book.

The home page is very much the front window of a website. When you come to create your own website it will be important that this element is particularly well designed and visually appealing. You will want any visitor to your site to be sufficiently intrigued so that they stay and explore further. The Web is a huge place and users are spoilt for choice: should your homepage be poorly designed, hard to navigate or just slow to load on visitors' computers, those visitors will move on somewhere else.

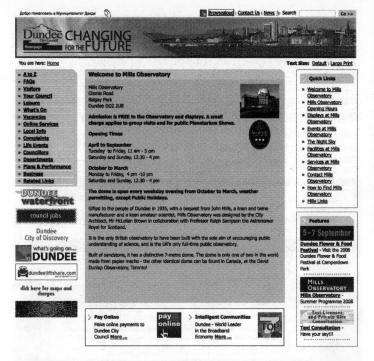

Figure 2.3 The home page is where visitors will begin exploring a site and where they will often return to following a tour of subsidiary pages

Headers and footers

Unless the websites that you frequent are particularly unusual, most of them will use headers and footers. To state the obvious: the header is the area at the top of a web page that is often common to most, if not all of the pages on a site. Similarly the footer is that area on the bottom of the page that remains constant.

To visitors these can be the 'safe' areas: no matter where a visitor may have navigated to within the site and no matter how complex those navigations may have been, they will know that they are still on the website that they originally visited. More significantly for them, buttons on the header and footer allow them to find their way back, should they become lost.

The footer is also used as a convenient location for all that useful information and those links that perhaps are not so glamorous as the main content. Hence you'll find links to the site map (a plan of the website), legal information, and even contact details.

Some web designers consider that producing a formal header and footer for every site can limit their creativity. That, to a point, is true but you will need to balance this against the benefits they bring for the visitor. Good web designers can also use familiar elements without them becoming clichéd.

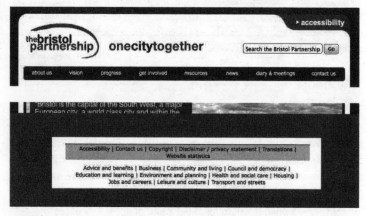

Figure 2.4 Consistency is a good reason to use headers and footers – as well as providing visitors with an easy route to the important areas of a site

Headings

Time was when websites were little more than essays and prose designed to be read much in the way of an onscreen book. Like pieces of work you might produce at school, each website began with a heading and might be broken up by the occasional subheading. The distinctly different header, which we discussed above, was still a feature for the future.

Now that websites are much more rich, in that they use photographs, illustrations, video and even sound, headings and subheadings are still important parts of a site. They help identify pages and let visitors quickly assimilate the contents of a page.

Remember that some visitors may be impatient and reluctant to read the entire contents of a page to find the section they want.

You'll discover later that when using headings on your page you need to be rigorous in the way you use them. There are two reasons for this. First, search engines (Chapter 12) will pick up on your headings and use them to index your web pages. Choose inappropriate headings and there's a chance that visitors will be incorrectly directed to – or away from – your website.

Second, and more significantly, HTML, the principal language used to generate pages, recognizes up to six levels of headings and subheadings. In fact, as almost all web designers will tell you, the best websites are those that don't use excessive amounts of text and, consequently, only essential headings and subheadings.

Body copy

The text on a web page that would typically be announced by, and broken down by headings and subheadings, is called body copy. Think of this as the editorial text in a newspaper or magazine. This is what you'll read when you first visit the site or a page. I've already noted that there should not be too much text on any web page; when creating body text – for whatever purpose – it needs to be carefully considered so that it is brief, succinct but still delivers everything that needs to be said.

Readability is essential. Poor grammar or wording will alienate your visitors so any wording needs to be well constructed. That readability can also be compromised by poor screen layout. Use a font size that is too small, a font that is not especially legible when reproduced on screen or a colour combination that is hard on the eyes, and visitors will turn their backs on the site – even if the words themselves are compelling. We'll look in more detail at these issues in Chapter 4.

Some websites, those featuring journals (blogs) or detailed stories for example, will necessarily need a large amount of body copy. In these cases, web page designers use subheadings, illustrations and even quotes (taken from the main body) to improve the readability.

The 48th Pennsylvania Volunteer Infantry/ Civil War Musings

An On-Line Journal Dedicated to a Civil War Regiment. . . plus some thoughts, reflections, rantings, ravings, and ruminations on America's fratricidal conflict from one historian/ranger's point of view.

WEDNESDAY, JULY 30, 2008

Schuylkill County Civil War Commemoration. .

As noted earlier this week, I will be participating in a days' long commemoration of my native Schuylkill County's Civil War history, which will take place in Pottsville in early September. More informtaion regarding this upcoming event can be found here.

Posted by John David Hoptak at 7:23 AM 0 comments

Civil War Interactive
CWi
Recommended Blog

Hector Tyndale: Fine China & Ceramics Importer, Philantropist, Abolitionist, and Civil War General

HELP RESTORE THE 48th PA MONUMENT AT ANTIETAM
Donations Sought To Replace Missing Sword From Statue Of Brigadier General James Nagle...
For More Information,
www.amonumentaltask.b
logspot.com
Or Contact John Hoptak:
johnhoptak@hotmail.co
m

About Me
JOHN DAVID
HOPTAK
GETTYSBURG,

Figure 2.5 Journal-based websites are heavy in text but use different devices to help break up that text

Hyperlinks and navigation

Generally abbreviated to 'link', a hyperlink is a place on a web page where, if a visitor clicks on it using their mouse, they will be taken to another page or location. As I mentioned in Chapter 1, this is Tim Berners-Lee's pivotal contribution to the Internet. This is an easy way to help visitors get around your site or to find additional information from sites that might be similar to your own.

To make it easy for visitors to see what is a link, they are usually picked out in a different colour (usually blue) and underlined. They will often change colour when you roll the mouse pointer over them and the pointer will change to a small hand symbol.

The blue, underlined text is now so entrenched in web design that it pays to stick with it unless there is a good reason to do otherwise. Even less experienced surfers will recognize these coloured words as links.

As well as individual words, websites will also feature navigation buttons that are also hyperlinked: click on these and the visitor will be transferred to the appropriate location. Images too are often hyperlinked. These may have blue outlines, and the pointer will, as with text, turn to a hand when over them. Clicking on an image may, for example, take you to another page or, often, will open up a larger copy of that image.

Hyperlinks also form the basis of site navigation. It's important to get around a site easily so you will often find hyperlinked navigational tools – buttons or words – arranged across the header of the site or, often, down the side of the page.

The example in Figure 2.6, from the popular Amazon website, features navigation buttons that instantly take visitors to the

Figure 2.6 The Amazon website is a good example of one that uses hyperlinked buttons and words to provide fast, convenient access to key departments

selected department of the store. To the left of the page are hyperlinked words, some of which mirror those along the top but provide quick access to other services offered by the site.

Searching tools

Many site visitors aren't visiting to browse, they are looking for something. This could be a specific book title or DVD (such as with the Amazon website) or it might be because they are re-searching a specific topic and a search engine has directed them to the site. It is not feasible to provide – on the home page – a hyperlink to every key element on the site (such as every book for sale) and so a search box is an important feature. A search box, often prominently displayed, allows visitors to enter the term or words they are looking for and have the website deliver to them a list of pages that correspond.

Convention – like that which decrees that hyperlinked words should be marked out in blue and underlined – usually places search boxes to the upper right of a web page. However, as search boxes tend to be somewhat obvious, such placement is rarely critical and should not compromise the layout of your web pages. It is quite simple to add a search box to a web page.

Media

Images, video and even music are now an integral part of the experience of visiting a website. Not so long ago the picture was very different, with the majority of sites being text only. That was dictated by circumstances: text-based pages don't require much data to be sent across the Internet and so, with the slow connections of those times, allow pages to be displayed rapidly.

- **Photos and images:** If you have ever edited digital images on your computer you'll be aware that the files that comprise these images are large – sometimes very large. Transmitting these over a conventional Internet connection would require a considerable time. To ensure images downloaded quickly they would be compressed and trimmed in size – to display on a computer screen, an image of much lower resolution than that required to produce a good quality print copy.

Today with Internet connections generally much faster these constraints are less severe; indeed, many photographers upload dozens of high quality images to photo printing websites rather than visit a conventional high street photo lab. For a web page though, you'll want images to appear almost instantaneously. To do so we need to optimize our images to get the best balance between quality and file size. We will discuss this process in detail in Chapter 8.

- **Video:** Even when images became commonplace on websites, video was still regarded a no-no. Video data files were substantially larger than image files and would be impossible for many site visitors to download. Again, advances in compression techniques (which make the video files much smaller without unduly compromising the quality) and Internet capacity now make it viable to include video on websites. Just think of those websites – such as YouTube – that exist only to deliver video. Producing – or converting – video for websites is just about as simple as optimizing images. I discuss this in Chapter 9.

- **Music and audio:** these don't enhance the look of a website, but they can affect the way it sounds. There are different ways that sound can be used to enhance a website, from providing background music, through narration of on-screen text (ideal for the visually impaired) to podcasts and more. Audio is becoming increasingly significant and so I have devoted a chapter – Chapter 7 – to using sound with your website.

Frames

Web pages are, conventionally, single pages similar to sheets of paper. There may be illustrations on a page and it may be large so that you have to scroll up and down it. Sometimes it can be more effective if a page is split, so that its parts can be moved independently. You might use this technique if, for example, you need one part of the page to remain fixed – it might have important text – whilst another part can be scrolled independently. Imagine an online photo gallery. You might want details of you, the photographer, to be displayed on the top half of the screen while visitors can scroll through a selection of your photos in the lower. Frames are often discouraged nowadays because they can present problems when using a search engine to try to find a website.

Forms

Many websites are passive; passive in the sense that they are designed for people to visit, read and enjoy but no more. Others are more interactive. They may provide information based on the type of visitor, and might want to recognize you, as a visitor on a return visit. Others may solicit feedback.

In order to do this the website will require that you enter information – personal or otherwise. You can harvest this data using forms. There is little difference between these forms and the type with which you are familiar with on paper (see the example in Figure 2.8). A form provides a series of blank spaces – called fields – into which you can add the data requested.

These fields can take different forms: some accept any type of input (any keyboard characters), others are more pedantic. For example, some fields will only accept numerical data – such as a telephone number – others may only accept e-mail addresses. Any entries typed in using the incorrect format will be rejected and the visitor prompted to re-enter the information in the correct way. Similarly, some fields will be determined as obligatory – where an entry is required, others are optional. For example, a name is usually obligatory where a date of birth entry optional.

Pop-up windows

Nothing attracts attention to a web page – or website – more than a pop-up window. This is a new window that opens on top of the home page (or, indeed, any other page) giving some important information.

Unfortunately, the pop-up window has been so abused – particularly by commercial sites which use them for advertising – that many web browsers (such as Internet Explorer or Safari) have user switchable controls that allow visitors to disable pop-ups wherever they occur. Many people now, almost by default disable pop-ups in their browser. So, rather than risk displaying

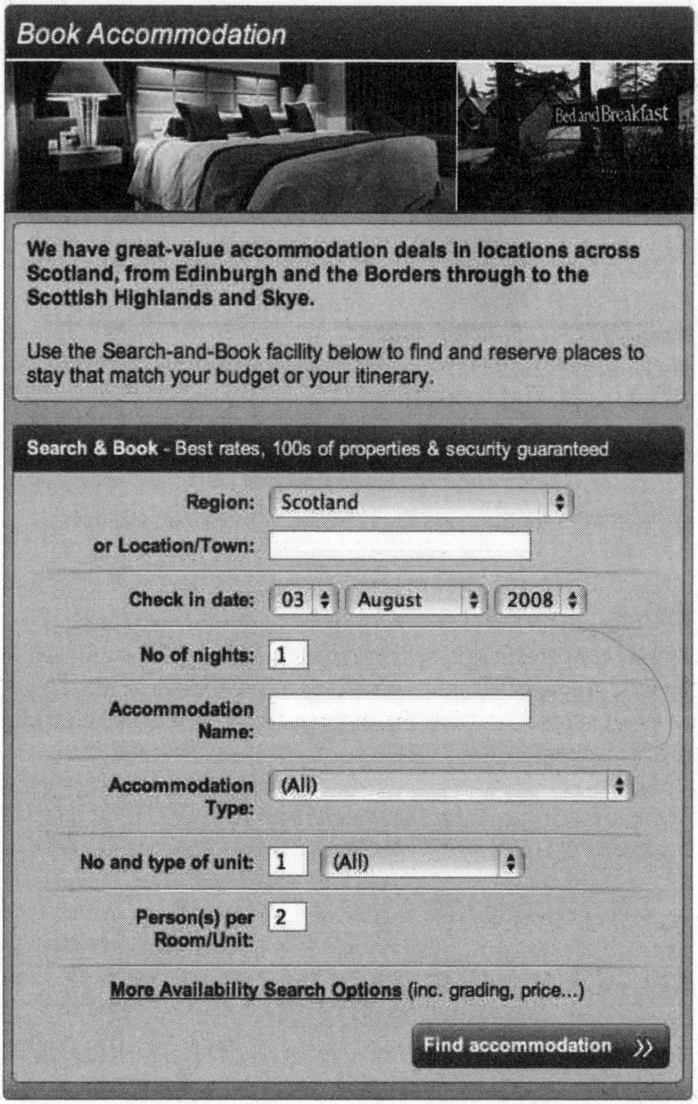

Book Accommodation

We have great-value accommodation deals in locations across Scotland, from Edinburgh and the Borders through to the Scottish Highlands and Skye.

Use the Search-and-Book facility below to find and reserve places to stay that match your budget or your itinerary.

Search & Book - Best rates, 100s of properties & security guaranteed

Region:	Scotland ⬍
or Location/Town:	
Check in date:	03 ⬍ August ⬍ 2008 ⬍
No of nights:	1
Accommodation Name:	
Accommodation Type:	(All) ⬍
No and type of unit:	1 (All) ⬍
Person(s) per Room/Unit:	2

More Availability Search Options (inc. grading, price...)

Find accommodation ⟩⟩

Figure 2.7 Forms will be familiar to anyone who has ordered a product or even a brochure from a website

important information on these, it's a good idea to give them a wide berth and, instead look at alternative ways of promoting those important points.

One such way is to have user initiated pop-ups. Though these look identical to conventional pop-ups they only open in response to an action by a visitor to the site. For example, when ordering from an online shop, a pop-up will appear questioning whether you want to proceed.

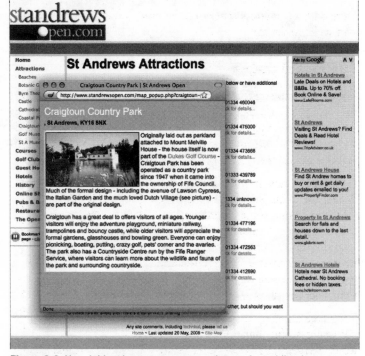

Figure 2.8 User initiated pop-ups are a good way of providing important information or alerting a visitor to their actions.

From web pages to a website

A website in its simplest form is a single web page. It may be a very long page but otherwise it's just something that is read – if text-based – or viewed (if comprising images) from top to bottom. A simple blog would take this form, generally with new entries into its diary format listed sequentially above older ones. There's nothing wrong with a site that is a single page but that page, as your content grows, can get unwieldy and navigating it even using the quick jumps that hypertext permits, can get untidy.

No, the best way to assemble your website is by breaking it into logical pages and then linking those pages together in a way that helps your visitors easily find the information, see the images or read the text that they came to see.

Here are four layouts that could be used – and actually are used – in website design.

Sequential pages

Imagine a web site that comprises one page after another in the manner of a book or magazine. When you read your way to the bottom of one page you could move on to the next. And when you get to the bottom of the second page, on to the third. This seems a sound idea, as it emulates conventional printed media.

However, it has serious drawbacks. What, for example, if the first page told you about some tantalizing information that was on page 27? You would have no option but to go page by page to page 27. Then repeat the process in reverse if you wanted to return to, say, page 5.

For small numbers of pages this layout might suffice but there are better ways. Sequential layouts don't really take advantage of the power of the Web.

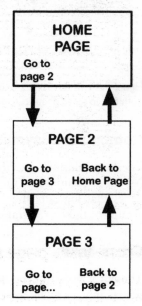

Figure 2.9 In this layout pages can only be visited sequentially

Hierarchical pages

One of those better solutions is the hierarchical page layout. Rather than a book layout, think of a family tree where the first page gives you the option of visiting any one of several different daughter pages. Each of those, in turn, allows you to visit daughter pages of its own. Now we can more quickly navigate to a chosen page.

This is a better solution, but still not one that optimizes the use of the Web or the most efficient to use. There's no option, for example, to go from one daughter page to (extending the metaphor a little further) a sibling page or the daughter page of a different parent.

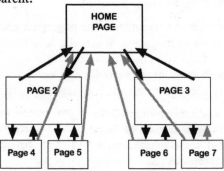

Figure 2.10 In this layout, pages can be visited more quickly but changing from one to a neighbour can still involve some unnecessary steps

Combination layouts

The best solutions are often compromises or, in this case, the best of sequential and hierarchical solutions. This allows those pages that logically follow on to be sequentially arranged but groups of these are arranged in a hierarchical structure.

Cross-linked (web) page

Though it does run the risk of getting a little messy, the cross-linked approach links each page with every other. You can jump instantly from one page to any other with no delay or intervening steps. Though ostensibly ideal, a site with a large number of

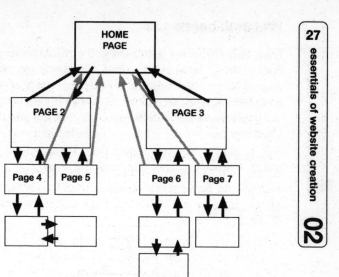

Figure 2.11 Combination: the best of both worlds?

pages can get unwieldy and the optimum layout will probably involve some cross-linked sections in an overall combination layout. The cross-linked layout is sometimes called a web layout but many people dislike the term 'web' here for the potential confusion it may cause.

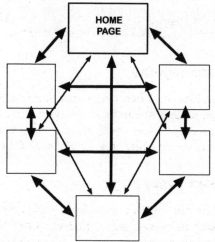

Figure 2.12 Cross-linked pages: in this layout every page is linked to every other

Which is best?

It's a case of horses for courses. It's probably very rarely that you'll select a layout that is precisely aligned to one of the categories above; in practice it is likely that parts of your site will include each type. Because of this it's vitally important that you, as a site creator, are able to map out your site and ensure all the links that need to be made are included and that your visitors will be able to navigate successfully. I will talk more about the site map when we come to design the website.

Summary

Through this chapter we have looked at the elements you will assemble to put your website together. In our analogy, we likened these to the doors, walls, windows and floors of a house. A good website, however, is not so much a house as a home. And if it is not stretching the analogy too far, a house becomes a home because of the personal features – decor, furniture and accessories – that we furnish it with. So it is with your website: in using those essential elements you need to design them in a way that gives your website its unique look and style. Now it's time to look more closely at the tools that allow us to express that style, taking our vision for the website and turning it into something that, in web terms, is more tangible.

03

software and tools

In this chapter you will learn:

- about the tools needed to create web pages and websites

- about different software packages

- about other useful resources for creating powerful web pages

With all the talk of HTML, sequential and hierarchical layouts, you'd be forgiven for thinking that my earlier assertions that website creation is simple was a bit wide of the mark. In fact, the fundamental process of creating any website is straightforward and involves just three steps:

1 Planning

2 Creating the pages

3 Post it onto – or publishing to – the Web.

Ensuring that this process remains simple depends on the tools you use. Many web design professionals do it the hard way – creating the most complex of web pages by using HTML code directly. That's not as masochistic as it might seem, given that there are tools that enable pages to be laid out with simplicity. It's because, by using HTML, you can create pages with greater accuracy and which are more robust (that is, with a lower risk of error) because they use very precise coding. Yet more professionals use products such as Dreamweaver that combine the best of HTML coding options with DTP style layouts.

Software requirements

Ask a website designer what software tools they would advocate and they'd suggest three main applications:

* **Web authoring software:** to create the web pages and website themselves.

* **Graphics editing software:** to create the images for your site.

* **FTP software:** to take the files of your website – complete with its images and graphics – and send them off to a chosen location on the Internet.

When you set out to create a website your options are probably dictated by two factors: budget and complexity. Ideally, you would want an application that makes it very simple to create a website but which costs very little – or is completely free. In practice you will find that there are, indeed, a great many free resources available on the Web. There are also many budget priced applications that offer creative tools of variable quality.

You can also opt for more powerful and competent applications but which come with a price premium. Those also make it easy to create websites but their substantial toolsets mean that they only flourish in the hands of experienced professionals.

Let's take a look at the options available from the budget prices (or free) through to those that a professional or serious web designer might use.

Budget priced web authoring applications

There's a very wide range of web authoring software available, from the free to the astonishingly expensive.

WebPlus

Sitting between these extremes are applications such as Serif's WebPlus. Now at version X2 (successor to the popular Version 10) this easy-to-use Web design application focuses on a desktop publishing-like approach to page layouts and requires nothing in the way of programming. You can choose themed templates to quickly produce your first website, and step-by-step tutorials guide you through the main stages of website creation. However, as your skills progress, it will allow you to directly edit the HTML code generated by the program and let you add your own new HTML.

Figure 3.1 Serif WebPlus: a comprehensive application at a bargain price

The later version of WebPlus also allows you to create and integrate blogs and photo albums directly, without the need to combine your web pages with those created by other applications.

You can also sell products online, as WebPlus includes all the tools that you'll need to create a shop within your website. WebPlus is a Windows product. Serif offer a special edition (SE) version of WebPlus that's remarkably well specified. Best of all it is free. I use it later for some examples.

Nvu

For another potent application that's completely free, take a look at Nvu. It's a web authoring package that's open source – that is, not owned by a company and one that anyone can contribute to the development of. This may seem laudable and altruistic but it comes at a cost: you won't find much in the way of technical support and development tends to be haphazard: at the time of writing official development had ceased in favour of a new product called Composer (see below). However, it is still possible to download the easy-to-use Nvu from the website: **www.nvu.com**. It is available for Windows PCs, Macintosh and Linux computers.

Figure 3.2 Nvu is a curious beast but effective and easy nonetheless

Mozilla Composer

From the people that brought you Nvu comes this updated Web authoring application that has been written from scratch to take account of the latest web technologies. It comprises part of the Mozilla Suite that also includes other Internet applications. Again it's open source and free, but it is probably true to say that it is still eclipsed in popular use by Nvu.

iWeb

Here's one for Macintosh users. It can also be considered as free as it comes as part of the applications suite on all new Macintosh computers and is also available as part of the iLife collection of applications (at an additional cost).

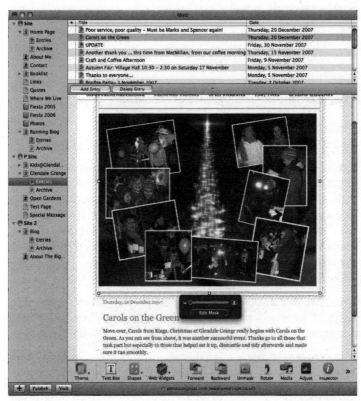

Figure 3.3 iWeb is true to the Apple ethos of ultimate simplicity of use

As a website and blog creation tool it shields the users almost entirely from HTML yet provides possibly the simplest way to build websites that can be media rich. It achieves much of this power because of its tight integration with the other iLife products such as image storage and editing application iPhoto and movie application iMovie. It gets better: iWeb also includes all the tools needed to deliver your website to the Internet, negating the need for a separate FTP application to achieve this.

Like the other 'i' applications there is some criticism that it does not extend its functionality to the level of an intermediate user (here because of the absence of HTML editing) but this is more than compensated for by the ease of use.

Professional grade software

When it comes to serious web design virtually every designer needs access to both HTML and all the other contemporary technologies. Programming directly in HTML is a great way of getting a web page just right but coding a large or complex website from scratch can take a great deal of time.

Dreamweaver

That's where programs such as Dreamweaver come to the fore. Originally created by web software company Macromedia prior to its acquisition by Adobe, this combines the best of the DTP style template-driven applications with HTML coding options. You could, for example, create a page using a layout view and then switch to HTML view to perform subtle adjustments and tweaks to the underlying code. The application also supports all the other key web technologies – such as CSS and JavaScript – allowing the user to capitalize on the options that these offer.

Dreamweaver also makes it easy to preview websites in many different browsers and debug them (that is, detect and correct potential errors and incompatibilities) relatively simply.

The program today is available as a stand-alone application or as part of one of Adobe's Creative Suites. These packages of programs bundle together other useful applications such as Photoshop (for image editing) and Illustrator for graphics design and allow components of the website created in these other applications to be seamlessly integrated into web pages.

This is all very neat and very effective but it comes at a price. Dreamweaver is designed for the professional and is priced accordingly. As Rolls-Royce salesmen are alleged to say, 'if you need to ask the price, you can't afford it': for one of the Creative Suite packages expect to pay well over a thousand pounds (or equivalent).

But, rather like its companion product Photoshop, the image editing application of choice for the great majority of photographers, Dreamweaver is the application of choice for many a web professional.

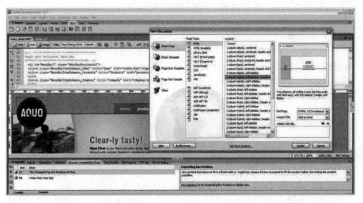

Figure 3.4 Dreamweaver's interface may look daunting but offers all the tools and options a professional designer demands

Alternatives to web authoring software

The focus of this chapter so far has been on dedicated web authoring software applications as the key tool for creating web pages. You might, then, be surprised to learn that you can use many word processing applications to create your pages. Microsoft Word and Works both allow you to save the documents you create in HTML format. Just about any document – complete with illustrations and photos if you wish – can be saved for the Web. You can also add hyperlinks to the page to help with navigation around the website.

Let's now take a look at other software that you will need – sooner or later – to satisfy your web creation ambitions.

Graphics and image editing applications

Though there are many sites that neither have nor need images or graphics, there's little doubt that some imagery can – when properly used – enhance a site. To be used on a website there are certain criteria that need to be satisfied by any image or graphic (and we will look at these in more detail later) and to best meet these you'll need an image editing application.

The exemplar for image editing, that we mentioned above, is Adobe Photoshop. This is a powerhouse of an application that really has no peers; there's nothing that you can't do with this compendious program. Like Dreamweaver, though, its professional market means that it is both complex to use and expensive to purchase. Difficult to justify for all but the most serious professionals.

Fortunately Adobe themselves recognize that Photoshop's technical requirements and consequent cost, preclude its use by the mass market and also offer Photoshop Elements, a trimmed down version. Actually, not just a trimmed down version, but one that is particularly user-friendly. Help routines, wizards and step-by-step projects make it easy to use even for the inexperienced. And, as for those features that are trimmed out, they tend to be the high end features that only the imaging professional would be likely to miss.

Better still, the latest versions of Photoshop Elements also let you produce photos and graphics for websites and, if you want to produce web photo galleries, allow you to produce these directly without the need to use any other applications.

Away from the Adobe stable, there are other competent image editing applications that are worth checking out. PaintShop Pro is a popular choice offering much of the functionality of Photoshop but at a much lower price. Serif, creators of WebPlus, offer a bargain priced but well specified application, PhotoPlus.

Before rushing out to buy any of these it's worth checking the software that came with your computer or (if you have one) digital camera. Often there's an image editing application provided in this bundle. The version may not be the latest and greatest, but for prepping images and graphics for your web pages it'll be more than sufficient.

FTP applications

Once you've created your web pages – or a complete website – the pages will still be sitting, like conventional documents, on your computer's hard disk. That's fine as a storage medium but to achieve your objectives of having these pages seen by anyone surfing the Internet you'll need to copy these documents to a location on the Internet. You'll also need a location on the Internet or, more specifically, on a web server (which is essentially a hard drive on the Internet optimized for handling websites) to install this software. I'll examine how you go about this once we've created some basic web pages, but to deliver your pages to this location you will need to use a File Transfer Protocol (FTP) application. These enable your computer to transfer files to and from a web server.

Today there is a wide range of applications to do this, some of which you'll find included with web authoring applications, some will be part of a package that you can buy from the people you buy your space on a web server from. And, of course, you can find some free applications by browsing the Web.

Planning tools

Planning your website is, as you will see in Chapter 5, key to creating the most efficient website and one that will meet your needs in the future as your site grows. Of course, you can rough out the layout of the site on paper – and it's often a good idea to begin this way. As the ideas for your site get more complex, though, you may need something more rigorous.

Many web designers, particularly those aiming to produce a comprehensive site, resort to using mind mapping and organiza-

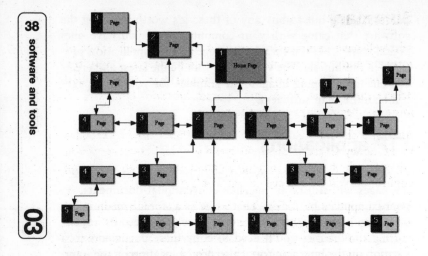

Figure 3.5 For determining and mapping the complex pathways of some websites, Inspiration is ideal – it even includes a website planning template

tional software. These allow you to visualize interlinked pages, update and modify the links and convert these layout diagrams into outlines. A great example of this software is Inspiration (www.inspiration.com) but there are many other options including some web-based free applications.

Plug-ins and modules

When you come to build your website you may want to include some special features. These may be as basic as a clock or calendar or as complex as a discussion forum. You could create these from scratch, using HTML. That, though, is rather like reinventing the wheel. Fortunately, for all these little add-ins, someone will probably have done all the coding already and chances are you will be able to find examples on the Web to drop them into your site. Sites like 1000 Website Tools (**www.1000websitetools.com**) are packed with useful extras for embellishing your site.

Summary

You will have gathered by now that there is a wide range of software and tools available to create web pages and websites. Some are all-in-one solutions that let you start from scratch and deliver the website to its final Internet location. Others focus more on specific elements of the process.

Also, you should have realized that you don't need to spend a lot of money. In fact, you could spend nothing! However if you are aiming high, an investment in a good quality web authoring application will be a decision you won't regret.

The best application for the web projects that you have in mind will depend, to a degree, on the type of website you will create and the 'look and feel' of that website. Clearly, a website that is substantially informational and text-based will need a different approach (and will benefit from different software applications) from a highly interactive visually compelling solution. In the next chapter we take a closer look at the design aspects before, in Chapter 5, we begin to create the website itself.

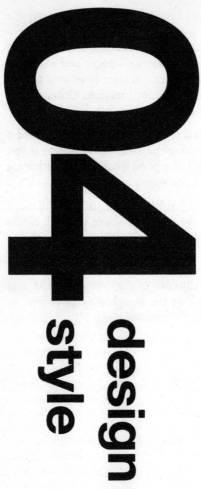

04

design and style

In this chapter you will learn:

- how to write effective text and copy for web pages
- which style and layout elements will be successful on a website
- how to link pages together to produce an easily navigable site
- about accessibility for visitors with special needs

By virtue of the ease with which websites can be put on the Web, there are huge numbers of sites vying for the attention of a growing but finite number of visitors and surfers. You've decided that you want to add your contribution so you will need to ensure it does not get lost or, upon launch, sink without trace. It's sad to say that the majority of websites are at best bland and in more than a few cases, downright mediocre. You need to ensure that yours stands out from this crowd – and does so for all the right reasons.

Spend a little time now, before committing anything to the page, deciding how you want your website to look. Consider also what type of experience you want for your visitors. Time spent in this preparation will pay dividends later, making it easier to attract visitors to your site and – assuming the content is up to the mark – ensure that those visitors hang around and return later.

Style or substance?

Back in the early days of the Internet and the embryonic Web, web pages tended to be rather prosaic. Mostly originating from academic sources, they were a way of disseminating learned papers and exchanging information. Like the technical journals they accompanied, the emphasis was on making the content of those papers widely available quickly. Scant regard was given to the presentation of the document and aesthetics were very much down the list of priorities.

Now things are quite different. We can do anything and everything when it comes to presentational styles. That has led to accusations in many quarters that some websites, desperate to stand out from the crowd, have put style well ahead of substance. Others have faced the equally valid criticism of putting style ahead of functionality.

Whatever the subject and purpose of your site, it is important that it is well designed. It should also place equal importance on the quality of content and the ease of use. Surfers today are spoilt for choice; if they are searching the Web they will not appreciate a website that looks good but proves difficult to navigate and cumbersome to use.

So, to avoid any potential red-flag issues let's examine the main elements that will comprise a website. Websites – and the software that helps you create them – give you pretty much free rein in how you use them but you will need to ensure that you follow certain guidelines. Whilst not cast-iron rules, they have been proven time and time again.

Words on the Web

Unless your proposed website will comprise only photo galleries or image portfolios, words – text – will play an important part in your website. Apart, perhaps, from an audio commentary (which isn't always practical to install on a website) text is the best way to convey information on a site and an essential component of any design.

Perhaps the biggest mistake newcomers make when producing text for a web page is considering the computer monitor to be the same as the printed page. Text will be entered and arranged exactly as it would on a page. Why is this a mistake?

First, a computer screen is harder to read from than a printed page. The brightness of the screen, perfect for many purposes, can be tiring when concentrating for extended periods.

Second, text produced for print does tend to be rather verbose. Not in itself a bad thing but something not so appropriate for the screen. Visitors to a website generally have less patience and don't want to read through largely-superfluous text to get to the key facts they are seeking.

Finally, the conventional layout of text for print doesn't always fit with the design of a web page where more succinct chunks of text – more readily assimilated – are more appropriate.

These issues become even more pointed when you consider that an increasing number of surfers and visitors to websites now do so using devices such as smart mobile phones or other handheld devices. With smaller screens, these devices are less able to display large blocks of text easily but are perfect for those more succinct paragraphs.

Incidentally, the image you add doesn't have to be the album cover – you can add any image. Should you wish – and we're a bit pressed to see a reason why – you can add several images to a track and click your way through them.

So far all our efforts and attentions have gone into getting music (and more) in to iTunes and into iPods. But you can also get your music out. You might want to produce your own audio mix CD, for example, or (should the worst happen) need to recover your iTunes library from your iPod

iTunes lets you create two kinds of music CD: an audio CD and an MP3 CD. Audio CDs are the conventional CDs akin to those that you might purchase at a music store. MP3 CDs feature music recorded as compact MP3 files rather than the more space hungry AIFF format used with conventional CDs. That means you can cram on up to ten times as much music as you can on a standard CD. The drawback is that not all CD players can play these discs; car CD players are the most likely to accept them.

As we've mentioned earlier when discussing backing up to CDs, you can't copy your library – or library items – directly to CD. Instead you need to create a playlist containing those tracks you want to burn to CD. It's a good idea, when doing this, to make a quick check on the number of tracks in the list, and the duration. As a rule of thumb, a standard CD will accommodate up to 15 standard tracks, or up to 75 minutes of music. The MP3 disc around 12 hours of music or 150 tracks.

To create a CD you will first need to visit the Preferences window and select whether you want the disc to be an MP3 CD or a conventional. In the case of the latter you can also specify a gap to be added between songs and whether to use sound checking. Sound checking is a useful feature if you've gathered together a selection of tracks from different original albums. It will ensure that the volume of the compiled CD is constant and you don't get tracks that are particularly loud or quiet.

Now you are all set to burn your disc:
- Begin by selecting the playlist you want to burn to CD. Check, as we noted above, that you're within the nominal capacity of the disc and that your compiled tracks are in the order that you'd like to hear them on the finished disc. If not you can drag and drop them into the correct order.
- Select File menu → Burn Playlist to Disc. Alternatively you can click on the Burn Disc button at the base of the iTunes window.
- Add a blank CD (if you haven't already inserted one) and wait for the burn.

It may take a little longer than you are used to when burning a CD. Whether you choose a conventional CD or an MP3 disc, iTunes will need to convert the files from the iTunes AAC format to AIFF (for a standard CD) or MP3 (for the MP3 disc). You will get visual feedback on the progress: keep an eye on the LCD panel at the top of the iTunes window to monitor the progress.

Once you've created you CD you might want to create an insert for the CD case. iTunes has second-guessed you and provides all the tools you need to make professional looking artwork for your new compilation.

To print your CD cover artwork select Print from the File menu. You'll see a dialogue box as shown in figure XX. The drop down menu in the dialogue provides a range of different styles for your CD case insert. You can choose a simple, text only insert or a colour mosaic that comprises thumbnail images produced from the artwork from the individual tracks. Make your

Figure 4.1 Large amounts of text on screen can be daunting for any potential visitor

Writing for a web page

Here are the points to bear in mind when creating text for your web pages.

• You're writing for the screen not the page. I have already alluded to the most important point: don't paste conventional Word documents to a web page without modification. Trim out anything that is superfluous and anything that is not essential. The main pages of a website are not the place to show off colourful literary styles!

• Short sharp sentences are preferable to longer rambling ones. Use bullet points to convey information even more concisely.

• Break long documents into chunks. You may have the most compelling content on your site, but if you present it as a single continuous piece of prose your visitors will take one look and move on. Yes, that may be their loss, but that's the reality of the Web. Instead, if you have a large document, break it into more manageable chunks. What's a manageable chunk? Consider that to be no more (and possibly a lot less) than a single screen full of text.

• It's best to link these chunks together on associated pages rather than make your visitors scroll down the page to each consecutive part. Remember too that some visitors to your site will have small monitors. So when you think about a screen's worth of text, that will mean something different for someone with a 15-inch monitor than it does to that design professional with a 24-inch screen.

• Avoid jargon. Unless you are writing for a specialist audience where jargon would be both understood and expected, keep to simple English. It's remarkably easy to use the odd word of jargon. You may think it adds to the gravitas of your site but, in truth, you just risk alienating visitors.

• Imitation is… There's that adage that imitation is the sincerest form of flattery so flatter the creators and designers of other websites by looking critically at the way they use text and the type of wording that they use and copy the ideas. Don't, of course, copy too much!

- Print it out! Okay, so I have just said that printed text and on-screen text are fundamentally different beasts, but printing the text you propose to use on your site lets you examine it more closely.

- On-screen text with the same scope as a printed document should have no more than 50% of the words. If you can trim further without compromising the content then so much the better.

Presenting your text

As well as getting your text in good shape compositionally you need to ensure that it is readable. The font – the style of lettering – you use and the colour (of the font and the background) can significantly affect the readability. Let's consider the font first.

Your computer can probably offer you tens if not hundreds of different fonts. Some of these are the basics such as Times New Roman or Arial – good general purpose fonts. Others are more extreme and downright wacky. When you come to preparing text for the Web you can never guarantee that surfers visiting your site will have the same fonts installed on their computer. In these cases, their computers will substitute a similar or generic font. If the layout of the text on your page is crucial, this can be a major problem.

So how can you avoid this potential pitfall? Use 'Web-safe' fonts. There are a range of fonts that are installed on virtually all computers and are considered as standard for Web use. Two of these are Times New Roman and Arial.

Times New Roman is a 'serif' type face, which means that the letters have small lines or flourishes at the ends of the main strokes. On the printed page this helps lead the eye from letter to letter and word to word.

This is Times New Roman   This is Arial

This is Century Schoolbook   This is Tahoma

Figure 4.2 Fonts: serif (left) and sans serif (right) fonts

Arial is a 'sans serif' font, which is one without the flourishes. Sans serif fonts are considered by some to be less easy on the eye in printed documents (compared with a serif font) but are often better for display on a computer monitor. The finite resolution of a monitor can mean that the detail of the serifs on the letters can't be accurately reproduced, leading to inconsistent results.

Other web-safe fonts include Verdana, Courier, Trebuchet and Georgia. What these have in common, often to the chagrin of the newcomer to web design, is that they are rather conventional and, compared with some fonts, dull. Not really very expressive. However this is no bad thing. Remember here that we are talking about the text used substantially for the body text of a web page. Here readability is paramount and it makes good sense to stick to one of these fonts. Not only are they likely to be reproduced accurately on all computers but they will be very readable.

You may want to break these rules for titles and headlining text. These are meant to be bold and stand out, but you still need to be wary of the font you use. Something too extreme may become unreadable if reduced on a smaller monitor or, if that font is not supported on a visitor's computer, will lose its impact.

THESE FONTS
are great fun...
...but can be
really hard to
READ ON A SCREEN!

Figure 4.3 Fun fonts: often found on the Web but rarely used successfully. Avoid!

Using images for titles

If you consider it important that you use a particular font for the title or you want to embellish the font in some way (such as giving it a shadow or glow effect), how can you do this without risking losing the effect on different computers? You can create your title in an image editing application and place the resulting image on your web page. In this way you can add whatever font, whatever embellishments that you want in the certain knowledge that any visitor or surfer to your site will see it in all the glory you intended. I will look more at handling images in Chapter 8. The same cautionary notes need to be applied though: don't go overboard. Because you can create and apply an effect doesn't mean you should! When we look, in Chapter 5, at building websites, you will see further options for combining text and images as headings.

Colour and font

Conventionally we display black type on a white background on our computer screens, emulating the look of print on paper. But it doesn't have to be that way. You could choose any font colour and any background colour. Black on white is the safe choice and the one that you'll find on most sites. Depending on your overall site design, though, it may not be the most appropriate.

Look around the Web and you'll see that basically anything goes in terms of colours. As you discover more and more variations you will come to appreciate that some combinations work and others don't. On the computer screen, blue or green text on an orange background can be hard on the eyes. So can purples and yellows. These combinations can be great for making a dramatic statement – drawing attention to a piece of text – but should not be used for extended paragraphs.

Text size

Just a note, before we move on, about the size of text. Consider your target audience and provide text of a size that is appropriate. Older visitors may struggle somewhat with conventional sized text and benefit from something a little larger. Accessibility of your website is an important consideration and one that I will look at more closely in a moment.

Formatting text

An often-overlooked way of enhancing the appearance of text is to format it more effectively. We are used to – in books like this, newspapers and magazines – large blocks of text divided only by the occasional heading and paragraph breaks. A more drastic style of formatting, with shorter paragraphs and bullet points for lists, for example, adds much to the readability and helps readers find their place if they glance away from the screen.

A word on accessibility

Though colour and font is something of a personal choice there is another angle to consider. The Disability Discrimination Acts in the UK put a demand on business websites that they should be accessible to the disabled. That means that they are easily read by those who have (principally) sight problems. It's a good idea – as far as is practical – to make your site conform to the same regulations.

A basic accessibility consideration would be to use clear fonts and colour combinations. Going one step further, you can allow visitors to your site to change the font (or at least the font size) and also change the font and background colours. Some people with sight defects will benefit from different contrast and colour combinations. Those with dyslexia too can often benefit where the option of different text colours is offered.

Though it surprises many people, websites can be used success-fully by those who are blind or have sight so impaired that they would be unable to read any screen in a conventional way. These visitors use special software that can read the contents of the page.

In practice, you would need to determine the level of accessibil-ity you provide or, with the tools that you have, are able to pro-vide. It is laudable to aim to offer as much as possible in this respect (and remember that the ultimate accessible site would accommodate the needs of the physically disabled and hard of hearing too) but if you don't have software that permits it, or your site might be compromised in some other way, you need to take a realistic and considered approach.

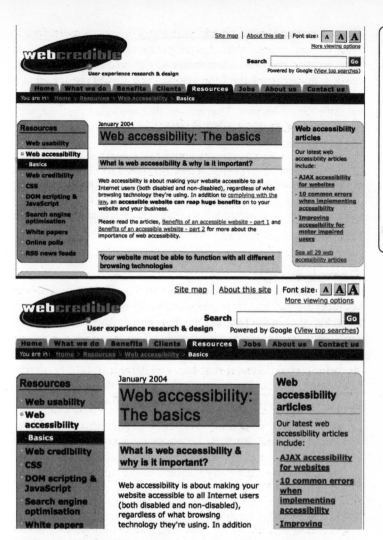

Figure 4.4 Accessibility considerations: some websites cater explicitly for visitors with different needs – such as user-selectable font sizes

Layout and style

In Chapter 2 we discussed the basic forms that a website might take, e.g. the photo album, the blog and the template-based. To a degree these will dictate its look and style.

The target market

Your website is a product, just like any other you may consider buying online or on the high street. Even though people don't have to pay cash to get to your site they do have to spend their valuable time with you. That means, like any other product, you need to assess your intended market and ensure your site is attractive to them.

A teenage fashion website is going to need a quite different approach – and quite a different look – to that of a model railway club. Similarly a website devoted to games and gaming is going to need a different approach to that of a financial services advice site.

Consistency

Let loose for the first time with a web authoring package can be a bit like that apocryphal child in a sweet shop. There are so many options that you can be inclined to make each page an explosion of contrasting colour and style. Believe me (and, better, believe your visitors) that this will leave any surfers utterly bewildered. Unless there is a good reason to do otherwise, you should adopt a consistent style and layout across your site. Here are a few of the areas you need to consider.

• **Colour scheme:** start off by choosing a colour scheme for your site. Colour will have the greatest impact when your site is first opened by any visitor. The colour, or colours, you select may be dictated to a point by the subject matter (clichéd, perhaps, but a gardening website is more likely to feature green and natural colours than pinks and purples).

• **An organized page:** most web authoring tools let you place objects – text boxes, images, or whatever, exactly where you want on the page. Some people like the opportunity this affords to create a casual random look to a page. To your visitors, though, this can just look messy. As you lay out your pages imagine a grid over the page and add your content to fit in with this grid. It may seem regimented and prescribed but this tidiness makes for a page that's easier to view. Keep the same format, as far as you can, from page to page. Your visitors will thank you as they'll know exactly where to go on each page to find the information (or type of information) that they want. Some web authoring software can help you by showing you grid lines and even indicating when the elements you are assembling on a page are aligned.

- **Fonts:** bear in mind the points already discussed and use a single font for all your main text with possibly a second font for emphasis.

- **Location and eyelines:** the position of the elements on the page can affect the attention that they attract. When a page opens on a visitor's computer screen their eyes will dance about the screen momentarily until landing on a key element of the design. In general, images will grab attention first, followed by headings and then body text. Elements towards the top of the page will generally draw attention first, and the top left gets the most attention.

- **Navigation:** last but by no means least, ensure you adopt an absolutely consistent style for the navigation system. The

Figure 4.5 The John Lewis website uses navigation buttons above a promotional image to provide access to all the main departments

places where visitors will go to navigate from page to page are crucial to making your site work. Visitors need to be able first to identify the navigation buttons and then use them successfully to move around the site.

Take a look at some of the most popular websites and, no matter what you think about the other design elements, they always have clear and consistent navigation buttons. Almost before you open the home page you'll know where to position your mouse to move to the section of page you are interested in. Bearing in mind that most people will look towards the top of the page first and many concentrate on the top left hand corner, these are the places where you'll most commonly find the navigation buttons.

* **Less is more:** finally, don't let your enthusiasm for your first website lead you into the mistake of cramming too much on to the page. Less is certainly more when it comes to web page design. If you've got a lot to say, or a lot to show, spread them across as many pages as necessary. Your home page particularly should be as clear and uncluttered as possible, offering a taste of what's in store and very obvious navigation buttons that lead to those treasures.

Figure 4.6 The Amazon.co.uk website uses a navigation pane on the top left. Like the John Lewis website, this pane is visible from virtually all pages that you navigate to, making it difficult to get lost

Getting around

Helping your visitors to get around is crucial to the success of the site. Providing all the navigational tools is a good start on this path but it needs to be backed up by a logical site design. You may have a large amount of information or resource on your site but it is down to you to make it easily accessible.

To consider the best way of arranging the information on the pages of your site, imagine you are a member of one of your target markets. What would they expect when they arrived at your home page, your virtual shop front? How would they find out – from this page – what information there is on the site and how would they access it? And how would they move around the site?

By asking yourself some simple questions like this and by noting down all the components of your proposed site you can begin to draw links between pages and between elements of the site. You can relate this to the navigation buttons and tools that you can use. Again, to see the optimum way of doing this, take note of what other websites do. Getting all the potential pages of your site linked together is easy, but to do so in a way that offers the most efficient methods to your visitors needs a little more consideration.

This is where it can be useful to refer back to the site anatomies discussed in Chapter 2. Some parts of the content may benefit from linear, sequential links between pages; others may be better with a hierarchical approach. There's no reason why your site should not use two or more types if it helps with the flow.

The three-click rule

There's something of an unofficial rule in web design that says that your visitors should be able to get to the information that they want (and here we're using the term 'information' loosely, to describe any result that they want from visiting your site) in no more than three clicks. So, whether they want to retrieve an archived article, send you an e-mail, find links to other websites or even buy something from the site's online store, they can do so by clicking on one, two or three links from the home page.

If you bear this in mind it can help you focus on what buttons you use for navigation. Take care, though, that you don't go to the other extreme. You could create a scheme where every single page of your site was accessible from the home page. In all but the smallest of websites such a regime would be so unwieldy as to be counterproductive. Visitors could indeed get to any page in a single click but would probably lose interest half way down the interminable list and opt to click away from your site.

The best way to achieve this optimally (and don't feel bound by the three-click rule; the odd four or five clicks to a particularly esoteric part of the site is no big deal) is to plan your website with four different page layouts, the home page, the content page, interactive page and intermediate page.

* **The home page:** consider this the shop window of your site. It gives a taste of what's within and the means – like a store directory – of getting to your chosen location. This is the page that needs to be as informative as possible, as attractive as possible yet as uncluttered as possible.

* **The content pages:** these hold the meat of your website. All that text you've carefully honed into shape, the carefully crafted photographs, graphics and, should the site demand it, movies and audio, can be found (or accessed) through these pages. How many content pages you'll have on your site will, of course, depend on the amount of content.

* **Interactive pages:** websites are not only places for visitors to find information, they also provide the means to respond to you or your site, or to other visitors. Interactive pages meet the demand for interaction, from allowing visitors to contact you by e-mail through to entering forums where visitors can exchange ideas, ask questions and meet.

* **Intermediate pages:** these are the workhorses of the website and provide the link between a page such as the home page and a content page. They are transitory pages guiding a visitor to his or her chosen final destination.

On a retail website, for example, the home page will provide the links to different departments: for example, books, DVDs, cameras and computers. Click on the DVDs option and you'll go to an intermediate page that gives you the options of DVD genres.

Search options

Of course, a sneaky way to conform to the three-click rule is to build in a search facility on your website. Then, from the front page your visitors can type in the subject that interests them and be shown a list of those pages that match – or be taken directly to the relevant page if there is only one option. On our retail website example above a visitor could avoid going from the home page to the DVD page to the 'Action' page and then through the title listing by typing in 'Indiana Jones' on the home page and getting a listing of all the titles that correspond to this search.

The site map

An important part of any website from both the perspective of the creator and the visitor is the site map. This is exactly what it says, a map of the pages of a website showing where each page sits in respect to every other.

Figure 4.7 The site map: when all else fails a site map can help a visitor find that elusive page

A navigational site map is an expanded view of the pages on a site based on the main navigation menus. An alphabetic site map – used on larger websites – lists all the pages alphabetically. In both cases it is usual to hyperlink the name of each page to the corresponding page, providing a quick link to it.

Summary

So, how could you summarize the approach to design and lay-out of a website?

The key attributes would be:

◆ Keep it simple.

◆ Make it easy to navigate.

Then:

◆ Get the words right – write for the web, not the printed page.

◆ Choose a legible font – and stick with it.

◆ Select a good, meaningful colour scheme.

◆ Establish a logical and consistent layout for your pages.

◆ Consider the needs of your visitors and any accessibility issues they may have.

Remember that time spent now at the planning stage will be amply repaid later. Choose an inappropriate layout, or get the interconnection of pages wrong when you begin building your site and you will spend a great deal of time correcting it later or, worse still, end up with a clumsy and unpopular site.

05

building your website

In this chapter you will learn:

- how to create a website using Microsoft Word
- about shortcuts and cheats for website generation
- how to create a website using a simple web authoring application

Were I writing this book just a handful of years ago, the contents of this chapter would be spread across several and, out of necessity, I would go into a lot of detail in regard to HTML, website constructional elements and the mechanics of building a site. Today, you can put together a website in minutes with all these mechanical aspects taken care of invisibly in the background.

Many of the sites you see scattered across the Web have been created by people with no knowledge of the way the Web works or how to produce a website. Indeed, just about all these people have no wish to know how the Web works or what happens behind the scenes. They have a story to tell, information and news they want to share. The Web is merely the vehicle. Before the Web made communication so simple, these people may have shared their information and thoughts by writing in books and would have done so with no knowledge of the mechanics of book publishing.

Today you can get on line simply by creating:

- a blog – an online diary

- a wiki – a collaborative information centre

- a photo gallery – a way to share images and photographs.

Because you can gain your web presence for any one of these in just a few minutes, you can concentrate your time and efforts on the content for the website. I will examine these alternatives in later chapters, but in this chapter I will look more closely at how to create your own website from scratch. Ultimately, you may decide that a blog or another pre-configured solution will better fit your needs. However, having an understanding of how websites are put together will stand you in good stead whatever option you choose. Fortunately, though, the path to creating a website from scratch is very similar: the software tools take care of much of the backroom design and configuration, letting you again focus on the content.

The Word option

Creating a website – whether a lavish corporate production or something more humble – is fundamentally about creating pages of HTML that can be posted to the Web. How you create that HTML will depend upon the ultimate objectives. If you choose to produce a blog or a wiki then the application software you use will create all the HTML and you will never catch sight of it. Similarly if you choose to use website authoring tools you will tend to work from templates and desktop-publishing style layouts. They too shield you from raw HTML.

One of the simplest ways of creating a web page is to use one of your everyday computer applications – Microsoft Word. Conventionally you will save your documents in Word format (where files are denoted by the file extension .doc) but Word will also allow you to save any page in HTML. How? Simply create your page as you would like it to appear on your website and, rather than saving it as a .doc file using the menu command **File > Save As > Web page (HTML)**. That's it. You've created a web page!

Figure 5.1 A simple Word web page

You can include text, illustrations and use any of the layout and formatting tools that Microsoft Word provides. As most people have at least a passing familiarity with Word it's an ideal way to create your first web pages.

Creating a Word website

The Word option is ideal if you don't want (or don't have) web authoring software or if your web publishing requirements are not too demanding. For simplicity, the example here involves creating a website with just a couple of linked pages. You can, of course, extrapolate this to create more substantial sites.

Step 1: Gather resources

Create a new folder and put any resources – such as images – in it. To make a website load quickly and to ensure that it doesn't occupy too much space on the Web you may need to optimize your images. (Chapter 8 goes into more detail about producing images for the Web.) You will also use this folder to place and store all the files produced for your website.

Step 2: Create your first page

Create a new document. Though you can save any document (even existing ones) as a web page, you can create a new document in that format (this is normally done by selecting a web page from the **New Blank Document** options, but this can vary according to which version of Word you are using and whether you are on a Mac or a PC). I'll call this *frontpage.htm*. The .htm – for HTML – extension is added automatically.

Step 3: Add text-based content

Though you are creating a web page, you can enter content – typing text, dragging and dropping images – in the same way as you would add similar content to a conventional document destined for print. Though you can begin typing from the top of the page, many web page designers who use Word choose to use text boxes to enter the text. This allows you to move panels of text around the page to improve the layout. Text boxes can also be resized to, for example, fit a space beside an image or put alongside another panel of text.

You can choose the font, the font colour, size and other settings for the text box just as you can for text typed directly on a page. You can also add background colours – useful if you want to use a text box for producing bold headings and titles.

Step 4: Add images

You can add images to any Word document; add them to a web page in exactly the same way. You can use the layout/formatting options to place an image:

* **In line with the text:** so an image is placed between lines of text, or between paragraphs.

* **In a square:** the image is placed in a square frame and the text flows around it on all four sides.

* **Tight:** the text flows around the image but close to the contours of the image rather than in a square frame.

* **Behind the text:** the image is place behind the text.

* **In front of the text:** the image is placed over the text.

Figure 5.2 Square formatting: this is often the most visually tidy

Transfer this material to digital video and we can give it a new lease of life, as we may well have done with analogue video recordings. Trouble is, movie film is one step further removed from the digital domain than analogue video and  the conversion process needs a slightly different approach.

Figure 5.3 In front of text: don't use this option unless you have a transparent image

Transfer this material to digital video and we can give it a new lease of life, as analogue video recordi one step further remov analogue video and the slightly different appro

Your first step should b had in store for so man this is to use an editor o one or the small hand driven devices once used to view and edit your movies. If you don't have one stashed away in the attic, you can find them on eBay or in many photo stores specialising in second-hand equipment. This is a worthwhile job for a couple of good reasons. After so

Obviously, visibility and readability is important when choosing how to use images. For example, the final option – in front of text – would obscure the text unless the image was transparent. Photos can be moved around the page, and also resized – smaller or larger – if required.

Step 5: Save your page

Word automatically saves your HTML documents just as it does any other format of document but, when done, remember to perform a final save. Make sure you save it in your web files folder, which you created before constructing your page.

Step 6: Adding a second page

To make an announcement on the Web you may get away with a single page. With a brief, succinct message to promote, a single page is the most efficient way to do it. However, chances are your web ambitions will be greater and you'll be looking at adding at least one more page. Create your second page in just the same way as you did the first, finishing by saving it in the same folder as the first.

If you open this folder now you'll see your newly-created page (which I'll imaginatively call *pagetwo.htm*) and *frontpage.htm*. You'll also see any images you've placed in the folder. Nestled among these files is another, one you've not created. It's titled *index_files* and has been created by Word as an index for your HTML files. There's no need to examine it – in fact it's better to leave it well alone!

Step 7: Connecting pages

If you were to publish these pages to a website now, you'd find a fundamental problem. There's nothing linking the two pages together. If you were able to see *frontpage.htm* on the Web you'd have no way of moving onwards to *pagetwo.htm*. To link the two pages we need to insert a hyperlink, a link that will allow us to access and read one page from the other.

Open *frontpage.htm*. You will need to place a link here. Imagine our *pagetwo.htm* is a set of contact names and addresses. On the first page you might add a line 'Contact Details'. You would want people to click on this to see the second page.

Step 8: Applying a hyperlink

To make 'Contact Details' into a hyperlink, begin by highlighting the text (as you would if you were planning to format it). Click on the **Insert Hyperlink** button.

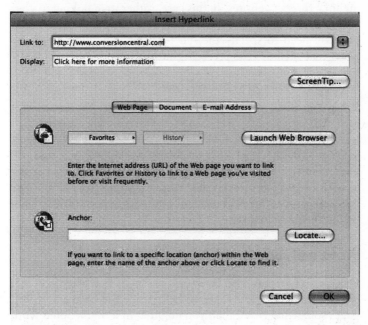

Figure 5.4 Insert Hyperlink button

In the dialog box, select the second page that you wish to link to. If your website contains a number of pages you can apply a several hyperlinks to the home page. It's worth referring back here to the topologies for websites (which illustrate the options for linking pages together) in Chapter 2.

You don't have to select text to create a hyperlink. You can select an image. Select an image by clicking on it and then click on the **Insert Hyperlink** button. You can proceed as described above.

Don't forget to include a hyperlink on your second page that lets visitors to your website return to the front page. You might want to include a line such as 'Return to Homepage' somewhere obvious on the page and provide an appropriate link.

Step 9: Linking outside your website

Interestingly, you can use this dialog box to specify any page, even those on other, published websites. So, for example, if you had created a website about cars, you might want to link to manufacturers' websites. In this case, rather than linking to your second web page, you'd link to that site. The caveat here is that you will need to specify the full URL, or web address, of any page: that includes the preceding http://.

Step 10: Check and publish your site

When you think you've got your site just right, you can view it as it will appear in a web browser. Double-click on your first web page and it will open in your computer's default web browser. You can now check whether the layout and appearance that you were aiming for when designing your site matches the appearance in the web browser. Once you've completed your site you can publish it to the Web. I'll look more closely at how to publish in the next chapter.

Word website cheats

Okay, so they may not be cheats as such, but Microsoft has provided a few little dodges to help make the creation of web pages somewhat easier than you might at first think. Some Word versions (including that in Office XP) feature a Web Page Wizard. Rather like a mini web authoring application, the wizard will guide you through the steps in creating a website:

- Step 1: create a title for the web page/site

- Step 2: set up the design

- Step 3: adding page types from a selection of templates

- Step 4: organizing and linking pages

- Step 5: add themes to define the look of the site.

The Wizard configures the structural elements of the website. You will still need to add the content and, when complete, publish.

Creating a website using a website authoring application

Some novice website creators avoid the Word option for web page creation under the misapprehension that the results will look rather like a Word document. Strictly speaking that is true, but that is because most of us use only a small part of what Word can offer in terms of layout and presentation. In fact, as I've already noted, a number of very proficient and popular websites are created with nothing more sophisticated than Word. Can you spot them? No, neither can I!

Word is first and foremost a word processing application. It is just fortuitous that the toolset has been extended to enable it to be used as a rudimentary website authoring application.

Proper website authoring applications differ principally in that all the tools needed to create a website are more easily accessible and offer a greater degree of control than the equivalents in Word. There are, of course, additional tools that will help you too. And, just as Word has web tools, so a website authoring application has word processing features.

Creating a template-driven website

A website authoring application such as WebPlus, which we discussed earlier, is ideal for constructing your first website, or for graduating to if you've made your first website using Word. This is a great all-round application at a surprisingly modest cost for the latest X2 version. A slightly trimmed down version of WebPlus 10, WebPlus SE is also available as a free download from **www.freeserifsoftware.com**. That's the application I've used here – not out of any preference but purely because it's a good example of the genre; if you choose a different application you'll find the methodology very similar.

WebPlus, when started, gives you several options including the chance to start a new design from scratch or to use a design template. You can also choose to view tutorials and other help documents.

Figure 5.5 The start screen of WebPlus SE lets you start a new document from scratch or via a template

Without an existing site to work on, most people, even those with some experience of creating websites, will opt for using a template as the basis of their new site. Templates are assembled by web professionals and represent good practice with regard to design. So why try to go one better, especially if you are not too sure what 'better' is?

Let me outline the steps you would take when using a template in an application like WebPlus. Like most creative applications there is no right or wrong way to approach a project so you may discover, as your skills develop, alternative ways to create your own website.

Step 1: Create a new site

Click on **Create site from template** from the Start-up Wizard. This opens a Templates pane from which you can make your selection. Choose one and click **Open**.

Serif use a template called 'Interior Design' to illustrate how to use their templates. Why? Because amongst a very good set of templates this is a particularly effective one, with good navigational tools ranged down the left-hand side of the page.

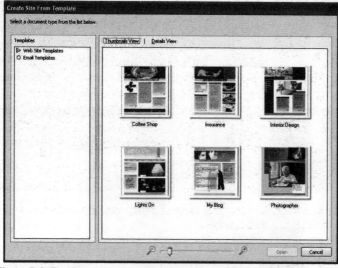

Figure 5.6 The Create Site from Template dialog box. Choose your template from here

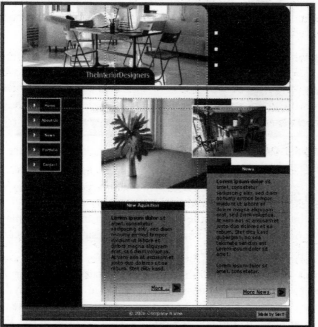

Figure 5.7 You are free to edit any of the components in a template

Step 2: Tour the site

In the box to the right of the screen, the Site tab shows the pages of the website that have been created. You are free to change these later but the default list is Home (for the home page), About Us, News, Porfolio and Contact. Click on each and you will see the corresponding page displayed in the main window.

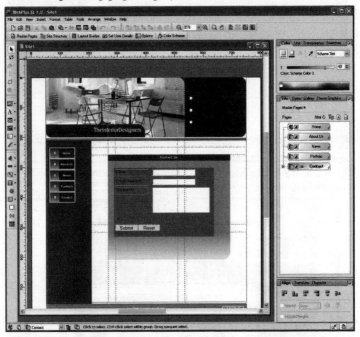

Figure 5.8 Click on the Contact button in the Site dialog box to see the Contact us forms page

Step 3: Editing a page

Let's begin by altering the title of the website and the images. Click on the banner heading 'TheInteriorDesigners' to select that box. It will open a dialog box called Flash.

In this template Flash (which we will discuss in Chapter 9) is used to supply the graphics. You don't need to know anything about this other than how to edit the wording. Click on the item **Company Name** and add the title for your website in the **Value** box.

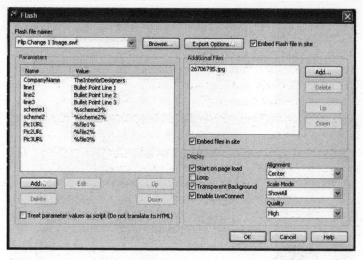

Figure 5.9 The Flash dialog box

You can edit (or delete) the other lines used in this template as you wish. You can, for example, change the bullet points in the heading and add a new image. For a new image, use the **Additional Files** pane in the dialog box and add the new images from any that are on your computer.

Step 4: Editing pages and placing images

The changes to the banner affects what Serif describe as a master page, that is a page (or a page section) that is common to all the other pages. To populate the web page you will need to fill each of the individual pages that are in the template. You may also decide that you need to change or add to them.

Let's begin filling the pages by clicking on the **About Us** page in the Site dialog box, then click on the **About Us** text box on the template to make this active. Select the current text using your mouse and press [**Delete**] to delete it.

Type in your text. There's a conventional word processing toolbar above the template window that will allow you to format and arrange the text as you would in a word processor. You can resize the text box if you have more or less to say than the space permits.

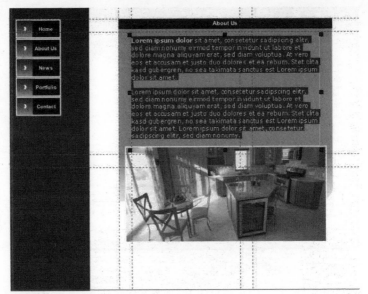

Figure 5.10 Select the text in any text box to delete it ready to add your own words

Next, double-click on the image to change it. It will open a dialog box from which you can make your selection.

Step 5: Modifying the web page layout

Unless you are very lucky (and not too ambitious in your website plans) the template layout of pages will not match that of your proposed site. You can add – or remove – pages from the site using the '+' and '–' page buttons on the **Site** dialog box, above the **Pages** panel. Rather obviously, click on the '+' page to add a page and the '–' page to remove one. Pages are added below the currently selected one.

To modify the structure, click on the icon to the left of the add and remove pages icons to open the **Site Structure** dialog box. From here you can also add pages but also move pages around. For example, in Figure 5.12, a new page has been added and moved to a subsidiary position as page 9. The control buttons at the bottom of the dialog box let you move pages to any desired configuration.

Figure 5.11 Double-click on any image to open the Images dialog box to select an alternative image

Note that if you [Control]-click on any page in the **Site** dialog box you'll open the menu shown in Figure 5.13. This also lets you add or delete a page, insert a hyperlink to an offsite page, preview the page, add some HTML code and even give an estimate of the time for downloading the page to a viewer's browser.

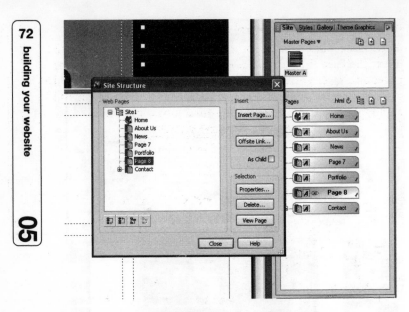

Figure 5.12 The add/remove page buttons and Site Structure dialog box are used to add and arrange pages in any configuration

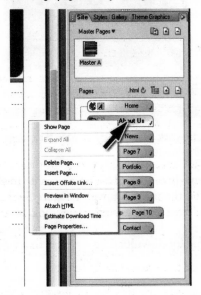

Figure 5.13 The Pages submenu

Step 6: Adjusting the page properties

Also on the **Pages** submenu is the **Page Properties** option, which opens the Page Properties dialog box. Here you can rename the page, and specify the name that will be used in HTML (you'd normally use the same name as the page). Here too you can add an audio file to play in the background (not compulsory!).

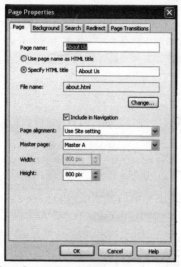

Figure 5.14 The Page Properties dialog box

On the **Search** tab you can enter a description of the website to be displayed when a search engine lists it in a set of results. Also you can add a list of words that a search engine will use to index it. In Chapter 12, I will discuss promotion of websites and you will see how important it is to add the right information here.

Those are the key stages for creating your pages and site in WebPlus. Even the SE version of the application contains much, much more in the way of features but, for your first outing it is important to stick to a basic toolset to get your site up and running.

As you set about creating your site, it's worth also getting to know the WebPlus set of manager tools, found on the **Tools** menu. The ones to note in particular are:

• **Scheme manager:** use this for a consistent colour scheme for all elements in the website.

- **Websafe fonts manager:** ensures that you use fonts that will appear okay in any browser.

- **Resource manager:** to manage all the images, video and sound that you might use on your website.

- **Text manager:** to ensure all the fonts you use throughout the site are consistent.

- **File manager:** manages all the files that you will use in the website and, when you publish it, upload to the web server.

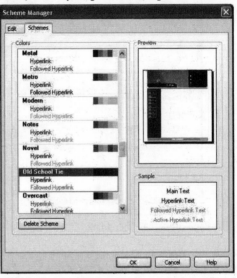

Figure 5.15 The Scheme Manager dialog box lets you select a predefined colour scheme for a site, or create your own

Creating a website without templates

The great thing about an application like WebPlus is that you can let it give you as much or as little help as you need. Templates give a large amount of support as you devise your first site but as your experience grows you will probably begin to appreciate what good design is and want to go it alone.

You could do so by heavily modifying existing templates or you can start with – literally – a clean sheet of paper. In this mode the application really does ape a desktop publishing application allowing you to create image and text boxes into which you can drop or type content, add tables, links and so on. Once you've used templates to create some pages you'll find your familiarity with the tools increases, and if you really do want to create something special, these tools will accommodate your every wish.

I must admit to being ambivalent about whether to work from a blank page or a template. I can draw an interesting analogy here with photography. It was not so long ago that photographers used cameras that needed a great deal of configuration before a shot could be taken. You needed to set an aperture, set the shutter speed and then focus the camera. Often a great shot was missed through either mis-setting any one of these or not getting them spot on. Plus, the photographer had to set up these and think about the composition of the shot he or she was taking.

Now almost all cameras offer point and shoot simplicity, with focus and exposure control taken care of automatically. The photographer can concentrate on getting the photograph perfectly composed with no worries about whether the mechanical settings are correct.

That's why I tend to recommend templates – shortcuts – wherever possible. That way you can focus on getting the content just right.

Summary

In this chapter I hope you will have seen that the creation of web pages and websites, so often apparently shrouded in mystique is actually no more difficult than creating a page in Microsoft Word (indeed, a page in Microsoft Word becomes a web page at the click of a button) or using a desktop publishing application.

So far you will have created a simple site – a collection of pages – but those pages exist only on your computer. They are not on the Web and only you currently will have sight of them. Next you will need to discover how to publish your website on the Internet. That is what I will concentrate on in the next chapter.

06 publishing your website

In this chapter you will learn:

- how to get a unique web address for your website
- about selecting a hosting service
- the pros and cons of free web hosting services
- how to upload your website

You've now created your website. The problem is, it is sitting on your computer and not available to be viewed widely. It needs to make the leap to the Web and you must provide it with a name that visitors can use to find it: you need to publish your site.

The three stages involved in this are:

1 Getting a unique web address name – URL – for your site.

2 Finding and selecting a host for the website – a company that will provide the web space for your site to sit upon.

3 Uploading (that is, copying) your site files to this location.

Once they are uploaded, you can then set about promoting your website so that your friends, families, colleagues and peers know how and where to find it. I will explore these promotional opportunities in a later chapter. Now let us concentrate on the process of publishing your website.

Getting a unique web address

The URL – Uniform Resource Locator – is the address which you, or your visitors, will type into a web browser to be taken to the website. It usually begins with www. and then features the name of the website, called a domain name. This will be in the form 'sitename.co.uk' for example, although the suffix '.co.uk' (the extension) may be different. Here are some typical extensions and their intended use:

.com	a commercial organization
.co.uk	a UK commercial organization
.org	a non-profit organization, club or association
.org.uk	a UK-specific version of .org
.gov	government departments and local government
.ac	universities and colleges
.sch	schools
.net	an Internet service
.info	site principally delivering information
.name	normally used for personal sites
.biz	a commercial alternative to .com

As you will have seen, some domain names can end in .uk, to emphasize that they are UK-based. Other countries use different extensions. Examples are .fr for France, .au for Australia and .ca for Canada.

There are some less well-defined country codes. For example, .tv was allocated to the Pacific island of Tuvalu but not all .tv domains are based in Tuvalu. The domain-name registry Verisign bought the right to sell .tv domains because of its value in implying a television connection. It's now used to denote domains of television companies such as www.five.tv, as well as those on the island.

When you are devising your domain name you may find that someone has already registered it. If 'yourname.com' is registered, you can see if an alternative such as 'yourname.co.uk' or 'yourname.net' is available. That name should be relevant to your site too: if you are running a club or association site you should aim to use one such as .org that reflects your status; a personal site might end .name. A commercial site would normally end in .com or .co.uk.

How do you investigate the availability of your chosen domain? You need to visit the website of an organization that handles website registrations. Examples in the UK include:

- www.ukreg.com
- www.names.co.uk
- www.1and1.co.uk

These companies can be found by entering 'domain names' in a web browser. The examples above were selected in this way – no favouritism is suggested and other companies are, of course, available.

You'll find if you visit one of these sites that they will offer a domain search feature. You can use this to check whether someone has already registered your preferred domain name. Enter your chosen name and extension in the box and press **Search**. Figure 6.1 shows a typical example, using my own name. It shows that most permutations are still available: the benefit of having a reasonably uncommon name.

Figure 6.1 Finding a domain: most domain registries offer a search function that will find out if your chosen domain name is available

Preparing to register your domain name

Once you've found a domain name that is currently unregistered you can go ahead and register it yourself. You'll see from the listing of possible domains using my name that several are free but that the cost varies between a modest £5.58 (for two years) for .org.uk through to nearly £60 for .uk.net. As a rule of thumb the most desirable command the highest prices (a .com more than a .co.uk for example) but be guided first and fore-most by the extension that is most appropriate to your site. Having the wrong extension (such as using .org in place of .com for a commercial site) can lead some visitors to think they are being misled.

Whois...?

If you're about to register a domain but are curious about who may own similar ones (for example, if you're about to register a .co.uk and you want to find out who owns the .com version) you can do so by visiting the UK registry, Nominet, at **www.nominet.org.uk**. Nominet offer the Whois service. Visit the website and type the domain name into the **Whois** box and you'll get full details of who owns the domain.

Registration

When you are happy with your chosen domain, discovered it is available and are happy with the price, you can go ahead and register. It's a straightforward process that you'll be familiar with if you have purchased anything from the Web. You just supply a few personal details for the registry and your payment details.

Web forwarding and e-mailing options

You'll probably find that you have some options to choose from as part of the registration (or post-registration) process. These include web forwarding and e-mail options.

Web forwarding lets you redirect visitors who type your new domain address into their web browser to another address. Why would you want to do this? If you've opted for free hosting space for your website (I'll shortly discuss this further) or you've set up a blog or a wiki, you'll probably find that you've a domain name that's anything but memorable. It wouldn't be feasible for anyone to casually remember the name. So you can advise them of your new, simple domain name and have them automatically forwarded on to your website.

The e-mail options allow you to set up an e-mail address related to your website. If your site is 'yourname.com' you can set up an address of 'info@yourname.com' or 'mail@yourname.com'. That's a great way of having an anonymous e-mail address and one that relates to your site. You can use it to allow visitors to leave messages or comments for you, for example. Any e-mails left for this address will be automatically transferred to one of your existing e-mail accounts, which you will need to specify when setting up this facility.

Selecting a host for your website

A web host is the generic term for any company or organization that provides space on their servers for your website. Some web hosts will also offer a domain name registration service and some registration services will offer web hosting, so the demarcation line between the two can, sometimes, get a little blurred.

Free web hosting

It is worth noting at this point – as you begin to consider the value for money offered by different potential web hosts – that some companies offer to host websites for free. Some even let you create your site from scratch for free. Using one of these, it's possible to build, develop and maintain a website with no outlay: no need to purchase domain names, no hosting fees and no consequent charges. Once set up, you can run and maintain your site just as you might one on a paid-for web hosting service.

Such free services can be a very effective way to get online if needs dictate that you do so at no cost. You might, for example, be producing a site for your family, a special interest or on behalf of a club or organization. You may not want to spend money on the development of the site or not have the funds. Is this a good option? The answer is, annoyingly, yes and no. Yes, because you can get on the Web at no cost. No, because there are drawbacks and restrictions. You will need to decide whether those restrictions would unduly compromise your website.

What do I mean by drawbacks and restrictions? Here are a few examples.

Advertising

Because the host of the site needs to make money somehow, they do so by selling advertising space. And that space appears on your web pages. That's often no big deal – surfers are used to advertising on web pages – but you've little or no control over what appears so you could find that the adverts don't fit well with your site. Imagine you're producing a website focusing on green technology and reducing carbon footprints. You could find it is supported by advertising for gas guzzling cars and airlines!

Fixed templates and layouts

The free hosts also offer free templates and layouts – often a broad selection, but still finite. If you want a unique look and feel to your site you may have few options beyond changing its colours. Experienced web designers can often pick out sites built from fixed templates and tell where the template came from. This may not be such an issue with visitors who are less likely to recognize templates and will be more interested in the content.

No access to the HTML

This may well be a bonus for anyone that never wants to get involved in HTML programming but, as your demands grow and your site expands you may find that you are prevented from altering the HTML. You'll be locked out of making some changes to your site.

Domain names

Getting to a website easily is often a key to its success. If your visitors merely have to type in your name suffixed by .co.uk, or .org.uk to get straight to your site you'll get (if your promotion of it is successful) a good number of hits. Free sites tend to offer a more tortuous URL of the form **www.freehostingsitename.com/ yourname**. Visitors will need to know that full name (and have a memory good enough to remember it) to find the site.

Fortunately, not all free hosting sites are so parochial in the way that they use URLs and many will allow you to direct visitors to the site from a domain name that you may have set up separately (as discussed in the previous section). However, to set up your own domain name you'd probably have to pay for the pleasure and so you'll end up with a solution that is no longer free.

No technical support

When you pay for a domain name for web space, some of the cost goes into providing a technical support service. The scope of this service may well vary between simple e-mail support to detailed telephone support. Either way it will be much more extensive than anything that free hosting sites offer.

Content

You may be restricted in the content of your site. You'll have no problem setting up a free site for a personal website, a family site, or most other non-commercial purposes. However some free sites don't let you operate web shops or sites that contain shops – or selling opportunities.

Locked in

When you create a website from scratch and deliver it to a hosting site you've the option – if you don't like the host – to move the site elsewhere. With a free site you're locked in and will be unable (or at best find it very difficult) to move it.

You'll need to carefully consider whether these are too restrictive. Work out how much it would cost to do something similar in a paid-for service and then assess the pros and cons.

Using a paid-for web host

If we are being pedantic, services such as blogs and wikis are free-hosted services. These, along with other free web hosting services mean that many people cut their teeth on such a service. There's no doubt that they offer a great way to get online fast and allow you to create some simple websites with no outlay.

However, if you consider the limitations are too restrictive then you'll need to consider a paid-for web host. If you have not found one already (as I mentioned, you can often get web hosting via the company you used to register your domain) then you can find many by using a search engine. As ever when shopping, do some research and compare what the companies are offering.

Here are a few of the questions you need do ask yourself:

* **What is the monthly (and other) fee?**

  You'll probably be expected to pay a fee for your space. Some web hosts will also charge for other services and may charge a set-up fee for setting up your site.

* **Can you use, or forward from, your new domain name?**

  Having set up your new domain name as something memorable, you want to be able to use it on your website. Not all hosts will allow you to use or forward from, your own name so make sure you check!

* **Does it allow you to use e-mail facilities from the website?**

  As above, can you use an e-mail address based on the name of your website?

* **How reliable is the service?**

  Web servers are remarkably reliable but do go down occasionally. Some hosts operate regimes that ensure downtime (when your site is not available) is minimal. Others (often the cheaper) make no guarantees. Most reputable hosts are happy to boast about their reliability.

* **What backup systems are there?**

  When a server fails – catastrophically – all your data could be lost. That means your website could be lost. True, you could then upload a new copy from your own computer but what are you paying your host for? They should, as part of their reliability regime, back up your website so that should a server fail, another with a copy can replace it fast.

* **What about technical support?**

  Setting up, uploading and maintaining a website today is straightforward, but all of us, at some time, will need some help. It's good then to know that your host has a technical support team ready to do so. But this can be where cheaper hosts save money, by offering just an extensive list of 'what if?' questions and answers in place of a real person. A good compromise is an e-mail-based system – you send an e-mail and get a response normally within one working day. Beware of some hosts who offer premium-rate support phone lines. Your modest monthly rates could soon be dwarfed by phone charges if you call regularly.

◆ **Are there any restrictions on the number of visitors (bandwidth limits)?**

This last point can be particularly important. You may find some web hosts will host your site for a very modest fee but will limit the bandwidth. The bandwidth determines how many visitors can visit each month and the amount of data that can be downloaded.

If you have a site that is mostly text information, that may not be a significant problem but if you have lots of images or video or even music that needs to be downloaded, that can eat into your allowance very fast. This means that either visitors will be restricted or you will be charged for using more bandwidth.

If you are creating a site rich in images and you want people to download these, or music or video is likely to feature heavily on your site, look for packages that offer good bandwidth.

Don't be afraid to question your potential hosts. They want your business!

Uploading your web pages

When you've determined which host offers the best service for your needs, you can go ahead and book your space. What do you get for doing so? Well, you'll get the web space obviously. You'll be given a password and login. These will let you access your web space for site maintenance. However, your website is still sitting on your computer even though you've now made space for it on the Web, via your host's web server. So, how do you get your website onto the web server?

Using an FTP client

Your host will probably have given you instructions and, if you are lucky, a few tools. One of those tools is crucial and is called an FTP client. This is short for File Transfer Protocol client – but all you or I need to know is that it's a program that's designed to easily move files (in this case the contents of a website) from one computer to another. You will be using an FTP client to transfer your website files from your computer to the web server of your hosting service.

If your web host hasn't given you an FTP client, don't worry. There are a lot of these available for download – many for free – on the Web. Others, offering better functionality, are available for a nominal fee. Names to look out for are:

- **CoffeeCup Direct FTP:** a particularly friendly FTP client (client just means it's the FTP software that sits on your computer) that lets you simply drag and drop files from one folder (that of your website) to the folder on the web host's server. Useful because it also has a browser tester to allow you to test your website on different web browsers.

- **Cute FTP:** another drag and drop style FTP client that is available in either standard or professional versions according to your uploading needs.

Note that some web authoring applications feature an FTP application either integrated into the main application or provided as part of a bundle of add-on applications.

Uploading

To upload your website you will need to know the address of the FTP server for the website (your host should have advised you of this), and the username and password for your website space on the host's server. Then you can copy – or drag and drop – your website files from your computer to the remote host.

Once this is done, and it shouldn't take very long, your site will be live. You can now use a web browser to navigate to the site and view it over the Internet. Finally, you'll be seeing your site as any other visitor might.

Checking your site

Just to make sure – and before you start promoting yourself to the world – try out your site using some alternative browsers. At a minimum, take a look using Internet Explorer, Safari and Firefox. These are the browsers that the majority of your visitors are likely to use. No matter how much testing you've done up to this stage it's essential that you double-check now to make sure everything appears as you expect it to.

As well as testing the appearance using different browsers, test all the links, to ensure that none have become orphaned or died. It can be easy, when tweaking your website prior to publishing, to compromise some links. You may have missed them earlier, but now is your last chance to fix them. Check too that other elements of your site – such as forms, e-mail windows, etc. all work as expected.

What if something is wrong? Correct it on the website version on your computer and upload the corrected, updated version. Some applications call this synchronizing – normally the remote site is always synchronized with that on your computer.

Summary

At long last you now have a website live on the Internet. You have good reason to be pleased: you've learned – and applied – a lot to get to this stage. But few sites are static. It's very sensible to build an initial compact and robust site but consider this as a solid foundation. Now you need to see how you can build upon this and develop your site. You can enliven your site with some major additions – such as movies or music – or something subtler – perhaps some illustrations and photos. You can diversify to include features such as user groups, forums, blogs and wikis. Over the next few chapters we will look more closely at these options and how you can best introduce them.

07

audio on
the web

In this chapter you will learn:

- how audio can be used on a site
- about including audio on a page
- how to create a podcast
- how to publish a podcast and
  have it featured in iTunes

A basic website can be eye-catching and, if the subject matter itself is sufficiently relevant, can hold the attention of visitors. However, most website builders realize that there's a lot of competition out there for those visitors, so it is crucial that your presentation is up there with the best. The design of the site lays solid foundations but other embellishments – such as the inclusion of images, video or audio resources – will also contribute strongly to your site's ultimate popularity. In this and the following chapters we'll look at these different media types, at how to incorporate them and how to best exploit the opportunities they provide.

Strong visuals – especially on the homepage – can be remarkably effective at grabbing the attention of a casual surfer who by luck or design has come across your site, and encourage them to linger. Sound too can be a powerful way of capturing visitors. In this chapter we will look at two aspects of audio on the Web. First, at how you can add audio to a web page. Second we will look at the increasingly popular medium of podcasting, creating audio narratives that can be added to a website or published directly to the Web to give an intriguing audio-only alternative to a conventional website.

Adding audio to a web page

Using just about any of the current crop of website authoring software it becomes easy to add audio to any web page. It is just a matter of specifying an audio file, where you want to place it on the web page and determining whether you want that file to play automatically (when the page is opened) or subsequently. In the latter case a visitor will need to click on a button to hear a message.

Although the process is straightforward, it can help to understand it better by looking at the mechanics that underpin the addition of sound. The process involves:

1 Uploading an audio file.

2 Linking to the file or embedding it in the web page.

3 Setting the playing conditions.

Uploading

This stage is normally taken care of automatically and involves copying the audio file to your website location using an FTP application. Traditionally the MIDI file type was the preferred audio format to upload but just about any common audio file format will work with today's browsers and delivery systems.

Linking to the audio file

Using this option a visitor to a web page has to make a conscious decision to listen to the audio file you've provided for them. Again, you probably won't see this stage if you are using a visual website authoring tool but it's useful to be aware of what that tool is adding to the HTML of the page.

Remember, in our example construction using WebPlus, all that was needed to add audio was to specify an audio file in the Page Properties dialog box. There was little additional control offered so it can be useful to have a basic familiarity with the HTML. This will allow you to make some adjustments to it later, possibly beyond what you might be able to do with your software application.

The HTML for the audio is:

```
<a href="filename.wav"> Link to Audio File </a>
```

What this brief snippet of HTML is saying is insert the audio file 'filename.wav' (in this case it is a wav format file). Where I have written 'Link to Audio File' is where you would add any message to a visitor to advise them of the file and where to click to hear it. See Chapter 14 for a basic explanation of HTML terms.

Embedding an audio file

Adding an audio file to a page is described as 'embedding'. When you embed an audio file on a web page you have the option of displaying a small control panel on the page for the visitor to control the sound, or making this player invisible. You can also have the option of playing the sound when the page has loaded or when a visitor clicks on a play button.

If you do add music using the embedding method and have it start to play immediately, consider those that don't want to hear it. Not necessarily because they don't like it but because they may be working or playing in an environment where sound of any sort is not welcome. In some circumstances a blast of sound, no matter how subtle or melodic, would cause visitors to quickly hit the Back button to leave. Make sure that you provide the option to turn off the audio easily and quickly.

Having music start straight away can also slow the loading of the website – or web page. Not as big a problem as it once was but still significant for some users with slower connections. Slow loading is sufficient reason for some visitors, admittedly the more impatient, to move on to another site.

When embedding an audio file, the HTML code will take the form:

```
<embed src="filename.wav" [attributes]></embed>
```

In the space indicated by [attributes] you can add certain conditions that describe the way the audio is played. For example:

```
autostart="true"
```

will make the audio file play automatically;

```
autostart="false"
```

will require an action from the visitor to play the audio;

```
hidden="false"
```

will make the on-screen audio control panel visible;

```
hidden="true"
```

will render the on-screen audio control panel invisible;

```
width="x" height="y"
```

determine the width and the height of the on-screen audio panel – typical values are 150 and 50 respectively;

```
loop="true"
```

will make the audio loop back to the beginning when the end is reached and play continuously;

```
loop="false"
```

will ensure that the audio track plays just once and then stops.

You may choose to use one, two or more of these attributes with the HTML but do remember that when using your authoring application the relevant HTML code will be generated automatically depending on how you wish the audio files presented. Don't be concerned if the above HTML code seems a bit obscure and apparently detracts from my contention about adding sound being simple. When you come to add a sound file using your web authoring application you will be well protected from this. Only if you need to perform modification outside what your software will permit do you need to venture into the world of HTML.

The audio player

Volume   Play slider   Review   Options
      Play/Pause   Cue/Forward

Figure 7.1

When the audio player is specified it will generally take a form similar to that in Figure 7.1. From left to right the controls are:

- **Volume:** a pop-up (or pop-down) volume slider will appear when this button is selected.

- **Play/Pause**

- **Play slider:** move this slider forward or backwards to move quickly to any position on the audio track.

- **Review:** press this to move backward along the audio track.

- **Cue/Forward:** press to move forward through the audio track.

- **Options:** This button may not be available if options (such as that to download the audio track) are not present. You may not want, for copyright reasons, to allow people to download the sound.

Podcasts and podcasting

At the risk of overusing the word 'simple', Podcasts are a remarkably simple way to get audio productions published on the Web. Podcasts are an audio narrative that can be integrated into a website. They can also act as standalone web-based resources. All you need to create one is a microphone, computer and an Internet connection. Once published, the audio can be listened to (and subscribed to, if you start producing regular podcasts) by anyone on the Internet.

In fact, you may well have already come across podcasts on sites you have visited or, more commonly via the iTunes Store. Here you'll find extensive categorized lists of podcasts that comprise radio shows, news and current affairs programmes, music news, corporate broadcasts and much more. The more personal podcasts are the audio equivalent of written blogs, with regular releases of news and views from the originator.

Unlike conventional downloads – such as songs or audio books – podcasts tend to be episodic: there may be a weekly or even daily release of a new edition. Interested listeners can gain easy access to consecutive episodes by subscribing, either at a website hosted by the creator of the podcasts or by using an aggregation system. This will check websites for new episodes. Apple's iTunes is the best known and most comprehensive of these.

Podcast practicalities

Podcasts also differ from other website content as they are designed to be downloaded onto the listener's computer for onward transfer to an iPod or MP3 player. Does a downloader of your podcast need an iPod to enjoy them? No. They can also be listened to directly on the computer they were downloaded to.

Create your own podcasts

Creating a podcast and publishing it, either on your own website or via a system such as iTunes involves these steps:

1 Preparing and writing a script.

2 Recording.

3 Editing the audio recording.

4 Publishing.

We could add to this list a final stage that includes promoting your podcast. The rules for this broadly follow those that I will discuss later with regard to directing traffic (a rather brutal term for visitors and surfers) to a website.

When it comes to the tools for creating podcasts, all you need in terms of hardware in addition to your computer is the afore-mentioned microphone. As ever, the higher quality this is, the better the final result. You also need the right software. My favourite is Podium by Softease (**www.softease.co.uk**). Ostensibly developed for the educational market, this keenly priced package is particularly effective in that not only is it simple to use but it can lead you step by step through the whole process.

If you are looking for a microphone, those offered by Samson (**www.samsontech.com**) represent good value for money and are particularly effective. Better still they can be connected to your computer – and powered – by USB. Nothing extra is needed.

Preparation

As with a conventional website the first step needs to be preparation. Collect all the material you want to use for your podcast. That will include a microphone, and one that will work with your computer. You don't need anything too complex or expensive. A simple model will be sufficient. In fact, if your computer comes with an on-board microphone you may find that this offers sufficient quality. Test it first though. Visitors to your website and listeners to the podcast can be demanding and something below par is likely to be a turn off – literally.

Produce a rough script. Whatever the content of your podcast, what you say needs to be well structured and well presented. Now, if you are using software such as Podium you can start it up.

1 Create a new project.

2 Fill in the podcast details. You need to enter the name you want to use for your podcast, your name as the author and, optionally, a podcast description. This information needs to be correctly completed, as it will be used later when your podcast is published.

3 Next complete the episode details: this will be the detail of the specific episode you are about to record. Podium assumes that, like most podcasts, this will be the first in a regular, semi-regular or occasional series. Any image you optionally add at this point will be displayed when you make the episode available on the Internet.

4 Open the script workspace: you can now build your script within Podium. You can also choose to create a multi-speaker if there is going to be more than one contributor. This is equally useful if you are using the podcast format to present plays or dramas. If you've already prepared your script in another application (such as Microsoft Word) you can cut and paste the text into the script workspace.

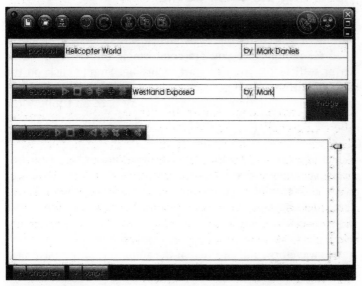

Figure 7.2 Scripting your podcast: details entered in the Podcast and Episode windows will, when your podcast is published, be displayed in iTunes

Rehearsals

Those with experience of radio presentation as well as podcasting will tell you how important it is to rehearse your podcast. For a start, a script that looks good on paper may not sound as good

– or flow as well – when read aloud. Begin by reading it out several times and rewrite anything that sounds clumsy. With a little refinement your script will match your reading style rather than your writing.

You can rehearse – whether alone or with other speakers if you have them – using Podium. To begin, click on the Play button in the script toolbar. In the manner of a television autocue system the text will be highlighted line by line and you can move through at an appropriate speed. Should you want a paper copy too (so that, for example, you can add your own cue notes and comments) you can print one off.

Recording the voice tracks

It's hard to say how long you need to rehearse. Some people are naturals and need just one or two rehearsals; others, me included, need far more. Once you are comfortable that you know the script sufficiently you can start recording. Simply click on the **Record** button. You'll get a countdown and then recording will begin. Take your time. Read at a steady pace and follow the cues on the script screen. Ignore the urge – common in us all – to forget all the rehearsing and rush headlong into reading the script.

When you get to the end, pause for a second or two and then press the **Stop** button. In a few moments you'll see the pattern of a waveform, which represents the recording of your voice. If there were multiple contributors, each voice will be shown in a different colour, corresponding to the colours shown in the script. Now you need to undertake your first check of the audio: look at this waveform and ensure that the amplitude of the waveform (the vertical height) is, at least on average, similar throughout.

If it looks okay, use the **Play** button to listen to your recording. Listening to your own voice for the first time you'll probably find plenty of mistakes – fluffs and poor intonations. Get a second opinion – and if there are too many gaffs you can just record the script again. Remember, even professionals need multiple takes to get things just right. Spending a modest amount of time here getting your audio perfect will serve you well later: listeners feel uncomfortable listening to a poor quality track.

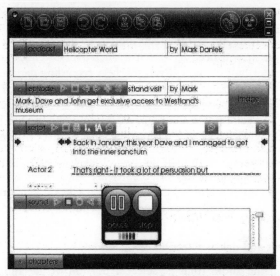

Figure 7.3 Lines of the script become underlined as a prompt as you work your way through. You can move from line to line by hitting the space bar

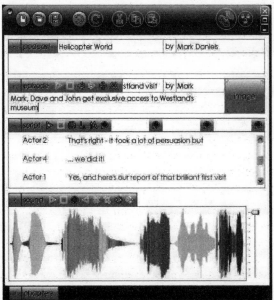

Figure 7.4 Audio waveform: at the end of the recording you will see a waveform similar to this. The average amplitude (height) needs to be similar throughout

Editing the audio

Once you're happy that the recording of your voice is as good as you'll get it, you need to give it a once-over to check for any other superfluous noises. Even the best recording can be compromised by odd noise – there's that time that you knocked the microphone in between paragraphs or the swoosh when you turned a page of notes. Or, perhaps, the microphone has picked up your sharp intake of breath at the start of your reading.

Podium provides sound editing tools that are rather similar to those you find on digital video software – and even more like the tools that you find to edit the sound tracks on video recordings. You can use these to remove superfluous noises and also you can:

• Select and delete a section of the audio.

• Crop the audio (that is, select a portion of the audio and delete the rest).

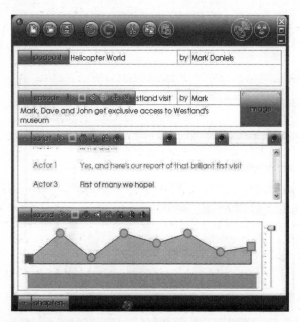

Figure 7.5 Audio editing: use the tools to modify the audio track by changing the levels or adding a second audio track

- Insert a piece of new audio or replace a section of an existing audio track.

- Alter the volume of a section of the audio – useful if one of your contributors was a little louder or quieter than others.

At this stage you can add an additional soundtrack too. Why? You might want some background music or sound effects. Adding them as an additional soundtrack means you can control and adjust these without impinging on your original recording.

Publishing your podcast

When you publish a podcast you make it available for anyone, in the same way as when publishing your website. In Podium you can begin the publishing process very simply by clicking on the **Publish** button.

You can upload to your own website but, if you want it hosted somewhere else or don't yet have your own webspace, Podium provides a location, along with all the information that you need to specify, to enable others to listen to your podcast.

Publishing and promoting through iTunes

After you've published your podcast you can let people know about it. After all, if no one knows it's there, you're not going to get any visitors! Start the process by clicking on the **Promote** button. This will allow you to share the unique URL address of your podcast through e-mail or documents.

To get a wider audience and to let more people enjoy your production why not submit your podcast to Apple and iTunes? The process is simple – or relatively so – and free. Though many podcasters can provide direct access to their podcasts via their own website, most now realize that iTunes is most people's first port of call when searching for those on their favourite subjects.

To submit your podcast begin by launching iTunes. This is installed as a matter of course on all Macintosh computers but available as a free download (from **www.apple.com/itunes**) for all Windows computers.

Go to the iTunes Store and click on the **Podcasts** link. Then, on the **Learn More** box click on **Submit a Podcast**. Follow the submission instructions on this page.

Figure 7.6 Submit to iTunes: having your podcast submitted to iTunes is not difficult and can give you a much wider audience

What happens next? When your submission has been made your podcast will go into a queue of other podcasts created by people like yourself, commercial organizations and special interest groups. It will, when it gets to the top of the queue, be reviewed by a member of the iTunes podcasting staff.

You'll shortly discover whether it has been accepted or rejected. Podcasts can be rejected for simple reasons such as technical (there's something wrong with the URLs or links provided) or practical (there may be password protections). In these cases just fix the problems (password protection is not allowed for the open access iTunes system) and resubmit. More problematic are the use of explicit language in the title or description, offensive content or misuse (or perceived misuse) of copyright material. Your podcast won't be listed if there is explicit language in the title (which everyone can see) or offensive material in the content.

Apple needs to be assured that there are no copyright violations in any of the content that you've submitted. You may have used (quite innocently) some background music that could be considered to be copyright and if you don't clearly have permission to use it, your podcast will be rejected.

Whatever reason for your rejection don't get downhearted; correct the problem (or modify any contentious sections) and resubmit. There's a lot of useful material about getting your submission through in the iTunes Help and on the Apple website.

Of course, most podcasts get through first time, and it's likely that yours will too. You'll be advised by e-mail and, within a week, your podcast will be listed by iTunes. Then, when you search through the podcast categories, you'll be able to find it.

Summary

You should now be aware of the basic principles and options of adding audio to a website. You will also be aware of podcasts, how to create them, and how they can be published. Although conceptually different from a conventional website, they provide an easy way to get a web presence in place of, or in addition to, a website.

08 images on your website

In this chapter you will learn:

- digital image basics
- how to prepare images for the Web
- about selecting the best images
- some simple techniques for creating your images

There's no doubt that photographs and graphics can enliven web pages and websites. Just take a look at any site and imagine it without pictures. We've already seen how easy it is to incorporate photos and graphics into websites, but it is worth spending a little time to discuss how you can ensure that you get the best quality and most meaningful images on your site.

Clearly this is particularly important if you are producing a photo album website, but everything you'll learn here is just as relevant if you plan to include a more modest number of images to support other aspects of your website.

Shooting photos

Before we get down to the preparation of images for the Web – Web optimization – let's take a quick look at the best way to shoot images for the Web and a few good rules to help you get those perfect shots.

Shooting with a digital camera

The most effective way to get photos ready to use on a website is to shoot them with a digital camera. That way you will – almost as a matter of course – be shooting images that can be downloaded to your computer. From there it's an easy step to prepare them for use on a website. You can also take the opportunity, equipped with the right software, to enhance any of those images. If you've only a conventional camera – one that uses film – don't worry. You clearly can't download your photos directly to a computer but you can – when you get your films processed – ask to get the images transferred to CD. That way you can use them on your computer in exactly the same way as if they'd come direct from a digital camera.

The general advice when taking images is that you should always aim to shoot at the highest possible resolution that your camera offers. The resolution – in case you're not familiar with the term – is a measure of the amount of detail recorded in an image. Digital cameras measure this by the number of discrete points at which colour and brightness information is recorded. A typical compact digital camera will offer a resolution of between four and seven million discrete points (called pixels) which is often sufficient to produce a colour print at least of A4 size of comparable quality to that from a film camera. Professional and top level cameras will offer more: perhaps 12 million pixels (12 megapixels) whilst even budget cameras today can command 3 megapixels.

Figure 8.1 An image with more pixels will render the same image at a higher resolution as this close-up shows

Does this advice about shooting at the highest resolution apply when shooting images for websites too? In general, yes. 'Shoot for printing not for the Web.'

This incongruous statement is one often heard when discussing how you should aim to shoot images for the Web. Why should you shoot at print resolution rather than the much lower web resolution? The rationale is that an image shot for the Web will be small and – though perfect for Web use – won't be usable elsewhere: it can't be scaled up to print or to be displayed on screen at a larger size. Shoot an image at even a modest print resolution of three megapixels and it will be fine to scale down for the Web. It will also be suitable for printing.

Images for the Web

So how do we prepare images for use on the Web? Preparation involves two steps:

* Modifying the resolution – resizing the image.

* Saving in a web-friendly image format.

Resizing an image

Because you don't need a high resolution image on a website you don't need to add one. In fact, it can be detrimental to have too many oversized images: large images will take up a great deal more space on a server, and image downloads will be more time-consuming than otherwise would be the case.

It is important that you resize your image so that it is appropriate to the use to which it will be put. What do I mean by 'resize'? It's changing the number of pixels in the image to (in this case) a lower number. You can do this by using image manipulation software – such as Photoshop Elements – though many web authoring software applications also include all the tools you need.

What size should you resize your image too? As a rule of thumb you can calculate your image size by allowing 72 pixels for every inch of the dimensions of the image (despite most other aspects having been metricated long ago, screen resolutions are still described in Imperial units). So an image you want to display on screen at five by four inches will need to be reduced in size to 360 × 288 pixels. You don't need to be too precise when resizing and it's okay to create an image that might be slightly larger than the calculated size.

In Photoshop, or Photoshop Elements you can use the **Image Size** command to set a revised image size, as shown in Figure 8.2. Once you've changed the size, give the image a new name when you save it – perhaps by adding 'small' to the filename. That ensures that you don't overwrite your original, larger image with the smaller version.

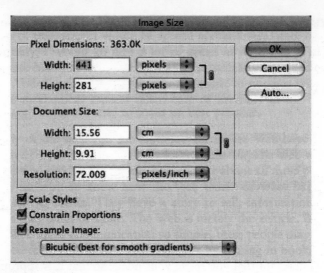

Figure 8.2 Use the Image Size command in Photoshop to alter the size of an image

File formats

We know it is important to reduce the size of the image to make it swifter to download to a visitor's computer. There's another dodge we can apply to make that download even faster, and that's by the use of the right image format. There are a number of different formats, each with slightly different characteristics and virtues. Some are designed to preserve as much detail as possible, some to be as small – in data terms – as possible.

The principal photo image format for Web use is JPEG. Short for Joint Photographic Expert Group (the group that determines standards) this format is also the one most commonly used for storing images on digital cameras – and so ideal. JPEG image files (often identified by the extension .jpg on the filename) are important because of the way they handle data. They use clever mathematical techniques to compress the amount of data needed to successfully record an image, by discarding a certain amount of it. This is data that is not judged as crucial to the image. The result is a file that can range from 80% down to around 5% of the original file size.

Back when digital cameras were relatively new and memory was expensive, the JPEG file format was adopted as a standard because it allowed (typically) around five times as many images to be stored on a given memory chip than would be possible using a format that did not employ compression.

Using the JPEG format means that the process of downloading a file to a visitor's computer is also massively reduced. Of course, there is a price to pay. The method used to discard data does result in a certain amount of image degradation. And the degradation increases as the amount of compression is increased. Compress an image to 20% of its original size and it will still look good; below 10% and you'll begin to notice some digital artefacts (usually blocks of colour) degrading the image.

It's a trade-off: fast downloads versus quality. A good compromise is usually achieved as, on screen, the digital artefacts are rarely as visible as they might be on a photo printed with the same amount of compression.

PNG and GIF formats

Apart from the JPEG format you may come across images and graphics that use the PNG or GIF formats. GIF format images can only display a smaller number of colours than JPEGs (256 versus 16 million). These are better reserved for simple images or graphics that don't need a wide range of colours and tones represented.

The GIF format is cherished by many web designers because GIFs can have transparent areas that allow the background image, text or colour to show through. Animated GIFs can also be produced: these are a series of GIF images that can be played sequentially in the form of a short animation, or animation loop. These can be used (sparingly) to attract attention to elements of a web page.

The PNG format is similar to GIF and was created to circumvent some copyright issues – now long expired – with the GIF format.

Figure 8.3 A JPEG and a GIF of the same image demonstrating the limited colour range of the latter

Changing image file formats

You can easily change one image format to another. Again, your image editing application will come to your aid here – simply open your image in whatever format it was created in and then use the **Save As** command to save it as a JPEG or GIF. When saving as a JPEG you'll generally be given the option of selecting an amount of compression to apply. Remember – more compression means a poorer quality image but that image degradation doesn't really become obvious until you've applied a very substantial amount of compression.

Selecting images for your website

Images add much to a website. Faced with a large expanse of text, no matter how compelling the content may be, the average visitor is likely to move on elsewhere. Add just a couple of images and the outlook is both metaphorically and actually quite different. Images grab attention and help break up the page.

Justifying images

But, and it's a big but, it is not sufficient to merely punctuate your pages with gratuitous images. When you add an image to a website there should be a rationale for doing so. For example, does the image:

+ Add to the impact of the page?
+ Help add to the information delivered by that page?
+ Reinforce the text?
+ Relate sufficiently to the text and context of the page?

If you answer 'no' to any of these, that does not rule out the use of the image but it might suggest that there is a better one that might be chosen, or that the text – or context – to which it relates could be modified.

You need to consider the environment in which images are viewed. A powerful image that looks good printed and displayed on the wall or in an album may not have the same impact when displayed in a small pane on a low-resolution computer screen. Simple, uncluttered images work best. If you don't have those images in your own photo collection then you need to investigate other ways of acquiring them.

Using old photos and illustrations

Imagine you are planning to produce a site with a historical slant: perhaps a site based around the history of your town or village or, maybe, your family tree. Chances are you'll have a lot of great resources that are photos from your (or other people's) photo albums. How can you include these on your website?

You will need to scan them using a flatbed scanner connected to your computer. If you don't have one yourself, perhaps you could find a friend who has. Or, if you anticipate scanning a large number of images, you might find it more economical and practical to invest in one. Don't forget that many computer printers today also feature scanners built in – the so-called 'all in one' devices.

Scanners create image files (and you can usually specify JPEGs) that can be stored directly to your computer's hard disk and used just as you would any other digital images.

Figure 8.4 A multifunction printer also features a scanner, ideal for producing digital versions of old prints and illustrations

Perhaps surprisingly, you can also get good copies of old images – certainly sufficient for website use – by using your digital camera to re-photograph them. To do this:

• Ensure that your camera is held square-on to the images you're photographing.

• Use a tripod or support to avoid any camera shake (unless the light levels are high).

• Avoid any reflections from the photo, or inconsistent lighting (such as light from a window) striking the surface.

• Use a close-up or macro setting to get the best focus.

Though a scanner will generally give you better results, you'll find that for the odd heirloom image, this can be a great solution. It's also a great way to capture images that you can't get your hands on – such as when visiting an exhibition or where it is impractical to scan an image. (But do remember when capturing other people's images, that you cannot publish them on your website without the copyright holder's permission.)

Figure 8.5 Scanned image: a scanned image like this is ideal for family trees and history websites

Buying images

If you're not a photographer, don't have a camera or you need some specific images for your site that would be impractical or impossible to shoot yourself, you can consider buying images from an image library.

Image libraries have been around almost as long as photography and for most of that time largely supplying the news agency and magazine market. Prices for purchasing images often reflected the intercontinental marketplaces and the esteem of the originating photographer.

With the burgeoning of desktop publishing and website creation a new generation of libraries have appeared that offer images at much lower prices and at a range of resolutions. So you could purchase a low resolution image for use on a website at a price proportional to the resolution. Two libraries to look at in this context are Fotolibra (**www.fotolibra.com**) and iStockphoto (**www.istockphoto.com**).

Unlike many of the libraries that cater for the business market, libraries such as iStockphoto put far fewer conditions on the use of the image, giving you more of a free rein to use it with your website.

Figure 8.6 iStockphoto has a wide range of cheaply available images on all subjects

Copyright considerations

That leads me on neatly to copyright. All images (and, for that matter, all text and other material anyone might create) are covered by copyright as a matter of course. That copyright, in the case of photos, normally resides with the photographer. So, any images that you've shot you can use as freely as you wish. Those you might have bought from a library will come with clearly assigned copyright. That might range from free, unhindered use to very precisely defined usage – for example, a single use on a single location on your website.

Image accessibility and ALT text

I have already made reference to the desirability of making a website accessible to those who have difficulties with reading or seeing a screen. I have also pointed out that severe sight difficulties are no longer an obstacle to visiting websites because of the screen reader technologies available.

If your website is heavily illustrated, or uses illustrations and images as an integral part of the site (perhaps with an image used in place of a formal text-based heading), those with sight difficulties may have particular problems even if screen readers are employed. To avoid this you can provide alternative text, or ALT text, for your images. This is special text that only displays (and would therefore be read by screen readers) when images aren't or can't be displayed.

You don't have to add ALT text to all images (and, indeed, it may not be necessary) but to do so on key images will make your site more accessible. You can add ALT text using your web authoring software. Or, if you know how, you can add it as a line of HTML.

Tips for shooting great images

The advice for shooting great images for use on your website is broadly the same as that for shooting great images generally but it does no harm to describe them.

◆ **Get the light right:** digital cameras today are adept at shooting in a wide range of lighting conditions from the brightest sunlight through to dark, evening and night shots. Make sure that you set your camera to get the optimum so that you don't get dark (underexposed) or over-bright (overexposed) shots. They'll look bad printed and worse on your website.

◆ **Sharpness:** most cameras now have autofocus systems that are great for taking away the worry of setting the right focus. However, autofocus systems are not foolproof (especially in low light conditions) and can often inadvertently lock on to, and focus on, the wrong part of the image. Double-check focus when shooting and discard any blurred images you might download. Sharpness controls in image editing software don't compensate for a blurred original.

◆ **Colour:** bold, punchy colours make for particularly effective and attention grabbing photos and none of this impact is lost on the Web. Try to avoid images that are too detailed and fussy and instead go for the bold simple imagery.

◆ **Composition:** where you place the subject – or subjects – in
an image can turn a mediocre shot into a great one and vice
versa. We all naturally tend to put the principal subject in the
centre of a photo but often this does not give the best look.
Use the Rule of Thirds to define a better composition. Imagine your viewfinder (or the camera's LCD panel) divided into
three, horizontally and vertically. Place your subject at one
of the intersections of the dividing lines to get the best result.

◆ **Test your image:** take a look at your potential images at the
size you intend to use them on your web page. Do they look
as good smaller? Could you crop your image (trim away the
edges) to make the subject have more impact? Could it benefit from enhanced colours? Would it look better if it were
presented in a square format rather than rectangular? These
modifications can enhance your image and are easy to apply,
as we'll see in the next section.

Figure 8.7 The Rule of Thirds is a great compositional rule and ideal for
adding impact to shots

Tips for enhancing photos

The great thing about digital photography is that it is easy to enhance images – making a good shot even better. Digital image manipulation tools let you do just about anything to an image, from the subtle to the extreme. There are shelves-full of books explaining every possible technique, but here is a succinct summary of those that will be most useful for your website images:

* **Colour and tone adjustments:** photos become more punchy if the colour is more saturated (that is, stronger). A beach scene becomes compelling if you make the sky a stronger blue and the water more aqua. You can enhance the colour using the **Hue/Saturation** controls. Increase the saturation slightly to give your photos a boost. Don't overdo this effect – the colours will become lurid and unnatural.

* **Colorized photos:** a variation on the Hue/Saturation feature is **Colorize**. Click this button (which appears on the same dialog box in your image editing application) and the image is converted into a single colour, toned image. It's an effect rather like the sepia prints of old, but you can vary the colour by adjusting the hue slider control. Colorized images are very stylized but can be more effective than a full colour image in many circumstances. A good case is when you use a similar colour for the colorized image as the colour scheme of your website.

Figure 8.8 The Hue/Saturation control lets you adjust hue and saturation and also 'colorize' a photo

♦ **Resizing:** I've already discussed the process of resizing; altering the number of pixels in an image. It's worth pointing out that you can increase the size of an image as well as decreasing; this is rarely (never) successful as a larger version will have no more details than a smaller one but take up much more file space.

♦ **Cropping:** cropping an image also reduces its size but this time it's by trimming off superfluous parts. Use the cropping tool to modify the composition, for example by cutting away featureless expanses of sky in a shot, or trimming away wasted space around a portrait.

Figure 8.9 Cropping an image removes superfluous elements and gives a more powerful result

♦ **Filters and special effects:** image manipulation applications are jam packed with filters. Unlike those photographic filters that are generally used on a camera lens to enhance photos as you shoot them, these filters are applied after shooting and tend to be more overt in their effect. As well as performing the duties of conventional filters, they can also distort, warp or convey painterly effects to your images.

Photographers often give these a wide berth as they tend to detract from the photographic virtues of an image. However, for the Web, it can be useful to reduce images to outlines or, for example, a watercolour. It's worth reiterating the earlier advice here, albeit in a slightly modified form: only use an image if it adds something to the page and then only add a special effect if that effect adds something to the shot.

Summary

Images can be crucial to a website but the selection of the right images is as important as preparing them. Casually insert an over-large image and your website will take too long to load. Choose a non-compressed format for saving your images and you'll suffer the same fate. But, with just a little forethought, it is easy to get great images that make your website stand out. In the next chapter we'll take the next step, into adding moving images.

09 using video

In this chapter you will learn:

- about video formats and media players for websites
- how to prepare video for the Web
- about Flash and other formats
- some shortcuts to getting video onto a website

Take a look at many websites and you'll be greeted – often on the home page – by a short piece of video. More so than images, video can provide an impressive entrée for your visitors.

Time was, not so long ago, that any advice about how to include video on your website would be prefixed by a warning: 'don't'. Until comparatively recently, the amount of data that needed to be transferred from a web server to a surfer's computer was so great that it could cause major problems, often resulting in failure to download or play.

Before broadband connections to the Internet became the norm, connection speeds (the speed at which data could travel to a computer) was too low to allow anything but the crudest video to be displayed. Anything larger would suffer from stuttering and freezing as the computer struggled to receive data and display it as a movie.

Second, many web hosting companies restricted the amount of data that a website could transmit over a given time period – and this often precluded the high-data transmission of video.

Last – but by no means least – video formats (how the video was converted to a digital signal) tended to produce very large files. The movie equivalent of a photo JPEG (a small file that preserved quality even when data was massively compressed) was still some time off.

Fortunately with broadband connections, higher data capacities and allowances for websites and more efficient file formats, adding video today should prove no more difficult than adding some good quality images.

Video formats and media players

Videos on websites are almost certainly of one of several types, playable using one of four media players:

- Flash Player
- QuickTime
- Windows Media Player
- Real Player.

Flash Player plays any Flash format video files. For most website creators, this is the format of choice, largely on account of all the replaying tools being virtually standard on most computers and with most web browsers. That means just about any visitor who comes to your site will be able to view the video without having to download or install additional software. I'll discuss Flash and the Flash format shortly.

QuickTime, from Apple, is the default standard player on Macintosh computers and also on some other devices such as the iPhone and many iPod models. It can also be downloaded and installed on Windows PCs. You can use QuickTime to play a number of movie formats including those with the file suffixes .mpg, .mpeg, .mov and .mp4 and others.

Windows Media Player is the Windows equivalent of QuickTime (in terms of media playing) with a similar range of playing options although older versions of the player will not be able to play some formats that are compatible with QuickTime.

Figure 9.1 The QuickTime media player will be familiar to viewers of web video

Adding video to a website

You need to consider adding video to a website as a two-stage process. Stage 1 involves preparation of the original video. Stage 2 is the uploading and installation of that video on the website.

Preparing video

What do I mean by 'preparing'? Well, the video may come from any of a myriad of sources. It may be that some video is in an ideal format for uploading directly with no further work required, but that's likely to be the exception. Chances are you'll have some video recorded on a digital camcorder, perhaps an older, non-digital camcorder or even – in the case of historic websites – on old cine film.

To get your movie in a suitable state to upload will therefore depend upon the original material. It will involve producing it in a digital format compatible with the website and, more to the point, visitors' computers. Here's what you'll need to do.

Cine film

Though it's perfectly feasible (with the right kit) to convert cine film to a digital format yourself, it's often easier and (for small amounts) more economic to have it done commercially. Many photo stores in the high street and on the Web will take your video material and convert it to a digital format, returning your original films along with a DVD with the digital copy. That digital copy can then be considered as a conventional digital source.

Analogue videotape

Old video tape recordings, such as VHS, Betamax, Video 8 or their contemporary equivalents may be video based but this video is analogue (that is, not recorded as a digital data stream which a computer can recognize). You can entrust the conversion of this material to a specialist company but there are a number of analogue to digital converters, or digitizers, that you can connect to your computer to enable it to do the job. Moderately priced, these can be a good option if there is a substantial amount of material to convert (such as an extensive collection of VHS material).

As well as allowing you to produce source video for your website you can also convert these old tapes to preserve the recordings – particularly useful for all those old camcorder ones.

Figure 9.2 Digitizers – A to D converters – are a simple way to digitize analogue video sources

Digital video

If you've a digital video camcorder (one that uses miniDV tapes, or records to DVD or memory cards) then you have video in a format that can be used – almost – directly. Why 'almost'? Well, you may need and probably will want to modify or edit it first.

Editing and enhancing video

With your video material in digital form (whether it was recorded digitally or has been converted from an older, analogue format) you will probably want to edit it before considering sending it to your website.

Unless you are very lucky, the video you have will not be perfect for adding immediately to the website. A raw recording from a camcorder is likely to be very long and contain a large amount of superfluous material. The video you send to your website needs to be as brief and to the point as possible. Think back to what I discussed about photographs: if you use them, they need to be good quality, serve a purpose as well as being optimized for the Web.

When you add video you need to ensure that it serves a purpose and that it delivers its point as swiftly as possible. Visitors to your site may be keen to see the key elements of the video but won't thank you if they have to sit through some irrelevant material first. Those visitors' legendary impatience will come to the fore and they'll probably give up on the video very quickly. If you have a mini blockbuster, don't stick it on the home page. Create a short – perhaps 15-second – trailer and put that on the home page. That will be enough of a tease for those who are interested to delve further and download the whole movie.

So how do you trim and edit your movie? You'll need some movie editing software. Macintosh computers come with iMovie which is a very competent movie editor – especially worthy as you get it for free. Windows users get (or can download) Windows Movie Maker which is a similar application to iMovie.

Figure 9.3 Applications like iMovie offer drag and drop simplicity for all aspects of movie creation

Both these applications are fine for most purposes, including trimming videos, assembling different shots into a continuous movie and splitting long movie footage into shorter clips. If you need something a bit more sophisticated (if, for example, video is going to comprise a very important part of your website) you could consider Adobe Premiere Elements (Windows) or Final Cut Express (Macintosh). Both are designed for the enthusiast video maker and priced accordingly, but do also feature some powerful tools found on the corresponding professional versions of each.

Video format conversion

Editing for the Web is, in general, a simple task and principally involves culling that superfluous material. The editing software can also save your edited movie in a format that will be more suitable for Web delivery. Just as you can save a Word document – using the **Save As** command rather than **Save** – as a text (.txt) or as an .rtf file, so you can save your movie in an alternative file format to that it was created in.

This is useful if you need to convert your original video into a specific format. To do so you can use the **Save As** command again and save to the required format. Unlike Word documents – or even photo files – that can be saved in a new format in seconds – saving video to a new format can take some time. Remember that a second of movie can contain up to 30 individual still shots so converting even a minute or so of video can take a good few minutes.

Using Flash for online video

Earlier on I mentioned that Flash was a common format for video on the Web. It's achieved this popularity largely on account of Flash video being relatively compact and that video being compatible with the majority of computers and computer systems. You may well have viewed a number of Flash videos, as this is the format that YouTube and Google Video use. That bit of news may start ringing alarm bells. YouTube videos are not known for their quality; in fact some are of very poor quality indeed. Does that make Flash a sound basis for video on your website? Don't worry. The reasons that many videos on YouTube look so bad are two-fold.

First, the original material used is often poor quality and may even be poor copies of an original. Second, YouTube hosts a huge number of videos. It can only accommodate these – and maintain its free status – by using compression techniques. As with the image format JPEG, overdo the compression and the quality suffers. This is the case on YouTube.

On your website you have more control over the quality and are unlikely to need to conform to the same constraints as YouTube.

It's worth noting some of the other benefits of using Flash beyond the aforementioned compatibility:

♦ **Small file sizes:** though, when assessing like-for-like quality, Flash video files are slightly larger than some alternatives, they are still very compact.

♦ **Screen size:** other video players often restrict the size that a video can be played; Flash gives the option to play at different sizes from a website, including full screen.

♦ **On-video watermarking:** you can place a logo or graphic on the video screen (rather like the channel identifiers you find on satellite and digital TV stations) that you can also link to the website. This prevents your video being stolen and, if it is, makes the original source obvious to any viewers.

♦ **More protection:** other viewers can easily allow a video to be downloaded to the computer of any visitor. This is not the case with the Flash player.

♦ **It will get even better:** two of the giants of video software, Adobe and Sorenson, are working hard on Flash to make it an even better format in the future. If it follows the path of other file formats, expect file sizes to become smaller and quality higher as time goes on.

Don't underestimate the compatibility issue. Many users, me included, don't like being dictated to, least of all by a website, over which software I need to install on my computer to view content on that site. I particularly dislike the Real Player format which seems to scatter little access files all over my computer. Get round this by using Flash and make the presumption that (virtually) all your users will have a great experience enjoying your video. What are the relative penetrations? They vary all the time but as a rule of thumb:

♦ Flash Player: 96–98%
♦ QuickTime: 45–55%
♦ Windows Media: 70–80%
♦ Real Player: 50%

Producing a Flash video

There is really only one problem with using Flash: you need to convert your video – whether or not you have edited or manipulated it – from its original format to Flash. Flying in the face of the general advice a page or two back, many video manipulation applications don't feature Flash amongst their collection of formats to which video can be output.

Using online video conversion

A sneaky way to do this conversion is to use an online service such as YouTube. You can upload your video to the service and they will effect the conversion from your original format. They will then host that video on their own servers, for anyone to take a look at. What, you may well ask is the point of that? You want video on your website, don't you? This is the really crafty bit: the online service does the work and provides the space for hosting (saving your own web space allowance) but also gives you a link and the HTML code for displaying the video on your website.

Here's the top four online Flash video hosting sites with their pros and cons:

- **YouTube** (www.youtube.com): first place of call for many video viewers, it suffers from the extreme compression I've already described. Although for your site this may not be a problem, there is a file limit of 10 minutes (or so) duration. That's why many videos on YouTube are divided into shorter segments.

- **Google Video** (http://video.google.com): though YouTube is owned by Google, the original Google Video service persists. It offers no (practical) limit on file sizes and will convert almost all original video formats. It also gives the option to either view or download videos (under the control of the person submitting). Higher resolution video is also possible.

- **Veoh** (www.veoh.com): good sized video with very little obvious compression, it also has no upload limits and a high data stream (a high data stream is capable of producing better quality video).

Figure 9.4 YouTube videos are plentiful but often of low quality due to compression

Figure 9.5 Sites like Veoh offer good quality video reproduction

- **Vimeo (www.vimeo.com)**: A weekly limit of 500MB applies, but this site also allows video to be stored in high definition format at very high resolution. All other sites currently support only standard definition video (like conventional television) and often provide even lower resolution.

DIY Flash video conversion

To have ultimate control over your video (though at the cost of a little more work) you can convert your video to Flash using a do-it-yourself approach on your own computer. If you think this route may be for you, take a look at the Riva FLV Encoder (**www.rivavx.com**), Windows or FFMPEG (**www.ffmpeg.org**), Macintosh. Both these can be used for free.

If you need something that delivers more control in the output video there are commercial applications available at all price points.

DIY or online?

This depends on your video. If the purpose of your website is to provide a vehicle for your video material, having it hosted on – say – YouTube as well as your own site brings you into the reach of potentially far more visitors. If you want to ensure that your video is prepared to a certain size or standard, then the DIY approach is for you.

It is worth mentioning, briefly, file compression. This crucial factor in photo and image file management is equally important for video whose files will be substantially larger. Often for Flash video conversion the compression is mostly automatic – little or no intervention is required. For the other formats (which I will discuss later in this chapter) you can, in the same way as a JPEG image file, specify the amount of compression. You can achieve that compression by specifying a lower resolution or by changing the data rate – the amount of data per second used to produce the video. Dialog boxes on the software let you select these parameters – among others – and will give a good indication of the final quality.

Playing Flash videos

To play your Flash videos on your website you need to install a Flash player on the web server. A simple job, and there are plenty of options available offering a range of controls from a simple start–stop video player through to more comprehensive controls.

A very popular example of a Flash player (or, more correctly, a website video player) is Wimpy Wasp, which you'll find at **www.wimpyplayer.com**. The idea of players like this is that they allow you to present and play Flash video files on a website directly, without the need for any additional programming or using any other software. Wimpy Wasp scores (for me, at least) in that it has a useful Customizer tool that automatically generates all the HTML you need for your project.

Figure 9.6 Wimpy Wasp is a great example of a Flash player for running video from your website

To use Wimpy Wasp to run a Flash video from your website, all you need do is:

1 Download the relevant files.

2 Upload the files to your website.

3 Open the Customizer tool and generate the required HTML, following simple instructions.

4 Upload the generated HTML.

It's worth noting that Wimpy also produce other players that you can incorporate on your website that can be configured to play a large range of audio and video content on your web pages.

Other video formats

Next in the compatibility hierarchy, after Flash, comes the Windows Media Player and the QuickTime compatible .mpg or MPEG 1 format. That means if your visitors have either of these players installed they are unlikely to need anything else. Disadvantages? It's an older format and less compact (for a given quality) than alternatives.

As we work down the popularity/compatibility list, the next entry and one of those alternatives is MPEG 4, denoted with the file suffix .mp4. This format was devised by the same group that developed MPEG 1. By taking advantage of technologies that had appeared since MPEG 1 was launched, the file sizes are smaller. It is also a scalable format, which means it can easily be used to store small video, such as that on a mobile phone, through to high definition broadcasts. The drawback is that Windows users will normally have to download QuickTime to view MPEG 4 videos. Similarly the QuickTime movie format .mov requires QuickTime to be installed or downloaded.

Audio Video Interleave (.avi) is a collection of file types (called by video technicians, a container format) that has a bias towards Windows-based computers. It is also the format used by some camcorders and many digital stills cameras when recording video.

RealVideo requires a Real Player be installed on any computer for it to be used. It remains a popular format but the simplicity and convenience of other formats make them more desirable, especially amongst recent waves of website designers.

Streaming video and progressive download

At the start of this chapter I discussed the early days of web pages when video was something of a no-no. When web video did begin to appear it suffered another drawback: it was often necessary to download the whole video file to the visitor's computer before you could start playing it. Given that download speeds were slow and video often of low quality, there was little incentive for visitors to spend a very long time (or so it would seem) waiting for that download to complete.

To avoid this waiting time, Web experts came up with the concept of streaming, where a player on the visitor's computer could play the video as it was being downloaded, so you could watch it almost immediately. To be effective, streaming needs special software and, often a special streaming web server. This does not make the technology user-friendly, so an alternative system called progressive download was developed. This too allowed a video file (or a music/audio file) to be played once sufficient data was downloaded. Then, assuming the data continues to be downloaded, playback can continue through to the end.

Figure 9.7 The BBC iPlayer

All the key media players (including Flash, QuickTime and Windows Media Player) allow video files to be played progressively as they are downloaded. Now we have become almost blasé about this and expect a video panel on a web page to start displaying immediately that page opens.

The process of streaming or progressive downloading delivers a copy of the file to the host computer but, generally, that copy of the file is not normally accessible. However, some systems allow the downloaded file or files to be reviewed later (the BBC iPlayer is an example).

It is worth noting that because the term 'streaming' was widely used, it still tends to be used nowadays to describe all video replays where the replay begins before download is complete, even though the term 'progressive download' is more accurate.

Summary

In this chapter you have seen that video can be included on a website as easily as images or audio. Like any resource there needs to be a good reason, a rationale, for including it – video files are large (even though compressed) and downloading data can affect the performance of a site.

In the next chapters I will look more closely at different website types. You will then get a better appreciation of where it will enhance your site to use resources such as video, audio or images and how you can best present them.

10

blogs and wikis

In this chapter you will learn:

- more about blogs and blogging
- how to create a blog
- what a blog can offer that a website cannot
- how to create a wiki

The blog is often described as the simplest form of website. Okay, some will argue that posting Word documents as HTML is even simpler, but a blog offers many of the features – such as multiple pages and interactivity – that many of us consider fundamental to a website.

Blogs have actually been around for a long time – or a long time in terms of the Web. The origin can be traced back to a time when Web contributors would put their diaries and journals online so that their peers and friends could share them. In those early days it often took a fair bit of Web knowledge to get a diary online, so it was not until the arrival of dedicated tools, such as Blogger, that the genre took off. These tools enabled those who would probably shy away from conventional websites to gain a Web presence.

Similarly, wikis, no doubt bolstered by the success of Wikipedia, are beginning to find favour in collaborative environments. Wikis can exploit the knowledge of a large number of experts who can contribute their know-how to the relevant areas of a single site.

Blogs and websites compared

Is it appropriate to call a blog a website? Some people argue that it is not. Why? They will point to the structure of a blog. Early on we looked at the different topologies of a website: the way the pages linked together. A blog tends to be linear: entries are added consecutively to form (after a number of entries have been made) a single, continuous page. Also, the structure of that page is such that, rather than having a front page, blog entries appear in reverse order, the most recent entry is at the top and is displayed when you first reach the site.

That, I would argue, is being needlessly precise; the fact that a blog lives on the same web servers as websites and substantially using the same infrastructure makes a blog just one type of website. In terms of impact, many blogs – particularly when it comes to those that comment on political issues – have become the most popular of sites and contribute much to social commentaries.

Content

So what goes in a blog? Anything you like. It might be a simple life journal, or it may be dedicated to a specific topic. Many popular blog sites gather a readership on the basis of the quality of the writing or even the (often opinionated) views of the writer. You are likely to find that a popular blogger may write about events in their life one day, air views on a particular bugbear the next, and comment on world events on another. It's this eclectic mix that makes them – for many visitors and readers – so compelling.

To make a blog truly gripping, though, you need to ensure that you add new material regularly – as regularly as visitors might reasonably expect – which often means daily or near daily. This illustrates two other differences between a conventional website and a blog. First, you don't refresh information as you might on a website – you add to it. The old material just moves, time-wise, down the list. Visitors who like your most recent entries are likely to want to read older ones too. Second, the popularity of the blog is in the addition of new material.

A blog community

More so than traditional websites, blogs tend to develop a community built around the content. Readers who visit and do so regularly will begin to comment on the stories (this interactivity, the ability to leave the blogger comments and to leave comments for other commentators, is another strength of the blog) and very quickly ideas and thoughts get widely shared.

Writing a blog

If you are considering a blog, either as a standalone or as an adjunct to another website, you will need to think first about what you want to talk about. Many blogs, as I have mentioned, gather a large audience and an audience keen to contribute themselves. However, for every one of these there are many more that are lacklustre in their content and, as visitors will attest, are not worth a second visit.

If you are going to create a blog that's going to be popular, you need to consider what you will talk about and how you will say it. Some popular areas for blogs are described below.

Community based

A blog that describes events, news and other issues that affect a community, such as your home town, village or estate is one of the more popular forms. It's a great way to disseminate information about a locality and will have a captive audience of other local people who will, should the information be relevant and frequently updated, provide them with a point of reference for that information.

To be successful, such a blog needs to be reasonably authoritative rather than partisan, but that does not preclude comments being left by visitors that address the points of view of others in the locality. Of course there are exceptions to this: you'll find that some community blogs are popular because they are controversial or because they support a cause that is at the heart of the community.

Family

Do you get – or send – those 'round robin' letters at Christmas, giving a detailed account of your family over the year? Well a blog is a contemporary alternative that people can tune into at any time. And, because you can write it at any time, it's likely to be a lot more thorough than a simple letter. Family blogs generally take one of two forms. A simple one just tells the story of one family unit for the rest of the extended family to read. A more sophisticated one can include events and news from the extended family, with comments, events and news also posted through the comment system of the blog.

It's feasible for there to be two or more prime contributors who can log on and add the main content, but it's usually preferable for one person to do this to maintain the style and integrity of the site. Remember that blogs can include photos and (depending on the blogging software you use) movies too, so it can be a great way to add movies of family events to share with relatives around the world.

Hobbies and interests

This is another successful genre for blogging. Hobby and special interest groups are frequent users of blogs because of the commenting and discussions that can follow the stories.

Travel

World travellers – of all ages – are beginning to realize that a blog provides the perfect medium to keep those back at home up to date on the progress of their adventures. Because it is relatively easy to keep a blog going – only needing some type of Internet connection – it's also easy to keep in touch and provide more detailed information than you might otherwise be able to send home.

Variations on the blog

As well as a standard, text-driven blog there are some alternatives including:

* **Vlog:** video blogs where video is the prime medium of the blog allowing contributions made on a webcam or other video camera system.

* **Photoblog:** one that's essentially a chronological photo album.

* **Moblog/mobilog:** one designed for viewing and sharing, or being written, on a mobile device such as a personal digital assistant (PDA) or a smartphone.

Creating a blog

The popularity of blogging has led to some great easy-to-use software appearing which, in turn, has led to even more people blogging. Today the most popular application is Blogger and you can find this at **www.blogger.com**. This is designed to be used by those new to blogging, new to website creation and, indeed, new to the Web, but that does not mean it's superficial. It is worth spending a few moments taking a look at how you can get going in Blogger.

Figure 10.1 Blogger is the most popular of blogging tools

Step 1: Creating an account

Before you can start blogging with Blogger you need to create your own personal account. This free process involves you entering a username, password, a display name (that which will appear on your blog) and an e-mail address. On a second page you will need to enter a general title for the blog and create a web address (URL). So long as no one has taken the name before, you can choose almost anything for this. Whatever you choose it will be suffixed by .blogspot.com.

Step 2: Choose a template

Though blogs, by their nature, tend to be a little prescribed in their overall layout, you can choose a template that will give your blog a modest element of individuality. It's worth looking closely at the alternatives as a blog can have quite a different character according to the template. Try to choose a template that is sympathetic to the subject: a classic design doesn't suit a blog on technology products whereas a cool green scheme can look good with natural subjects. Once you've chosen your template click on the **Continue** button to confirm your choice. You'll

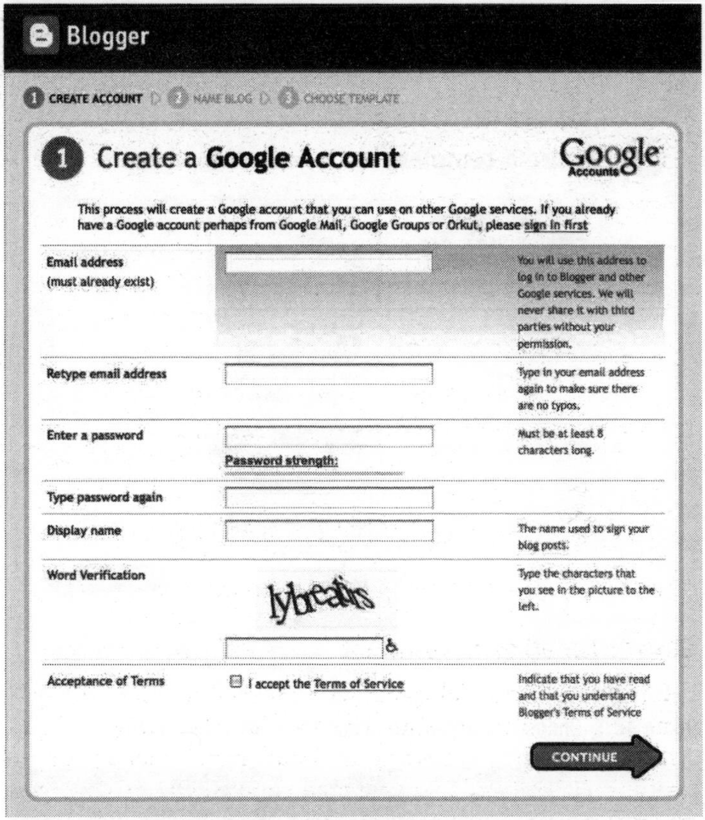

Figure 10.2 Start with Blogger by creating your account

receive a message telling you that your blog has been created. You are all set to go!

Step 3: Adding content to your blog

You can now start adding content to your blog. Click on the **Start Posting** button to begin.

Title your first blog and then begin typing your text in the main box. If you've ever contributed to a forum or a user group you will probably be familiar with the look of the screen for entering the text. It will allow you to enter your text and then choose a font, a font size and any other enhancements (such as bold or italicized text) you want to use. You can also select the colour of

Figure 10.3 Choose a template to match the style of your blog

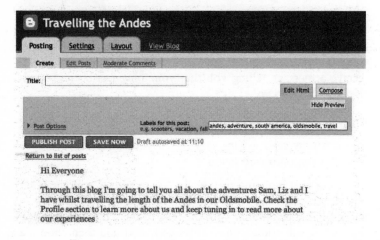

Figure 10.4 Creating your first blog entry is simple

the text and whether you want it aligned to the left, right or fully justified (aligned to the right and left margins).

Once you have entered all your text – or at any point while entering it – you can preview how the wording will appear in the blog. Click on **Preview** to do this. This will show you how your wording will appear – with all the modifications – although it will not show you that text in your chosen template.

When you are happy with your entry you can hit the **Publish** button. It makes good sense now to check that the blog appears as you expect. Click on the **View Blog** link. It's always advisable to do this even if you've previewed the blog earlier; sometimes gremlins can be at work and interpret your text in a different manner to how you expected.

Also you'll now see it with the template you've chosen, so if, for example, you've chosen one that puts a coloured background under your text, you can assess its legibility and, if necessary, go back and change the text colour to something that appears more clearly. Bear in mind what I said earlier with regard to accessibility. If you have text and background colours that are too similar in shade or contrast you (and your visitors) will have difficulty reading. It may be stylish, but it won't be readable!

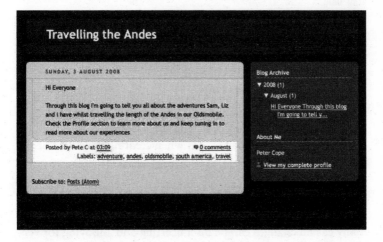

Figure 10.5 Check how your content appears with your chosen template

Step 4: Editing your blog

Your first entry is now complete and available for the world to see and read (or notionally so, as your potential visitors will need to know about it). You can now add additional entries – just as you would a diary – or perhaps edit your original.

When you are ready to return, visit the Blogger website and log in using the details you created when setting up your account. You'll now see the Dashboard window.

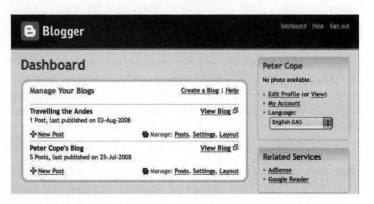

Figure 10.6 Blogger Dashboard: this is where you can edit and modify your blog

The Dashboard is where you will return to edit your blog, add new entries and change other information (such as your password). You can also set up a profile here, to give visitors some more information about yourself.

Click on the displayed link (which will have the title you added when creating). Your blog entry will now be displayed and you can click on the **Edit** button if you want to make any changes. Then you can proceed as you did when creating the entry for the first time.

It's good form not to change old entries in your blog too much or too often. It's okay to update information (especially if you highlight the part of the entry that has been updated) but too many casual changes can be disconcerting and annoying for visitors who will prefer to read new content and not have to check back for changes to older material.

Step 5: Adding a new post

Once you've made your first entry to your blog – and seen it live on the Web – you'll probably be drawn into making another entry. And why not? Blogs are designed to have new entries whenever you feel the urge or have something important to say.

Select the **New Post** button on the Dashboard and adjacent to the title of the blog entry. This will open the text input window and you are free to add new content. Finish by publishing your blog and taking a look at the new entry to ensure it looks okay.

Step 6: Adding images to Blogger

Though blogs began as a way of sharing written information and views conveniently, nowadays – with the proliferation of digital cameras and digital images – people are just as keen to share photos too. After all, if you are maintaining a family blog there will be many photos of events that you'll want to share.

To add an image to a Blogger entry you need to open, or have open, the blog entry to which you wish to append the images. Click on the small image icon on the header of the text entry box.

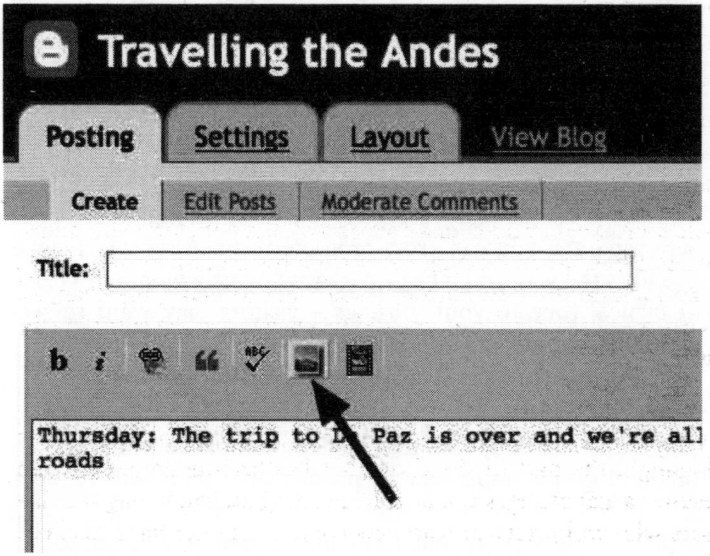

Figure 10.7 Click on the image icon to add a photo to your blog

A new window entitled **Add an image from your computer** will open. This lets you select an image to add from your computer or, by entering a URL, anywhere on the Web.

In this window you will also need to choose a layout (whether the image appears to the right, left or central to the text) and the size of the image: small, medium or large.

Browse for your selected image (or enter the URL) and then select **Upload Image**. After a short period (as the image file is uploaded) you'll get a message confirming that your image has been uploaded. You can now go and view your blog with the image included.

Don't worry about how large the image was originally, prior to uploading. It will be optimized and resized to conform to the layout of the blog.

Step 7: A second blog

Creating blogs can be infectious. You might have noticed that the Dashboard allows you to create another blog. You can use this if you want to create a second, discrete blog. You might want to do this if you want your postings to address distinctly different subjects. You might, for example, be producing a blog for local community topics but also want to share family or hobby information. A single blog containing entries on both will not read well for those interested in only one topic as they will have to wade through irrelevant material to find things that interest them.

You can create as many blogs as you wish. Though they are all kept separate, you can cross-promote them. After all, if someone likes the way you write – perhaps you've a wonderful ironic or cynical tone to your musings – visitors may want to read what you have to say about other topics.

Step 8: Adding contributors

Though I've already said that having multiple contributors to a single blog can sometimes be problematic, there will be occasions when you will want others to help you out. Other family members, perhaps, or other committee members of the society whose blog you maintain.

Do this by opening your blog, selecting the **Settings** tab and then clicking on Members. Here you will see the option for adding additional contributors, or team members as Blogger calls them.

Click on **Add Team Member(s)** and type in the e-mail address of the new contributor. You can do this for several contributors at the same time and also include a message that will be e-mailed to them when you click on **Save Settings**.

Blog Authors Your blog can have up to 100 authors.

> 1 Author can post to this blog
>
> Pete C   admin
>
> **Invite more people to write to your blog**
>
> tomsmith@condenast.com
> davelewis@sekcom.co.za
> mharris2009@lutronics.com
>
> Enter the email addresses of people you want to write to your blog (separated by commas).
>
> INVITE   CANCEL

Figure 10.8 Complete the e-mail fields to add the e-mail owners as contributors

Step 9: Linking beyond your blog

As your blog is a website – albeit of a specialized form – it is on the Web and can therefore be linked to other sites and pages on the Web in the same manner as any other website.

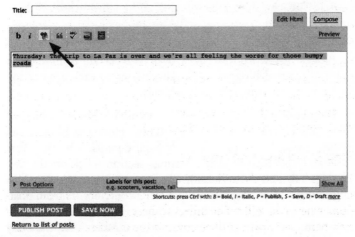

Figure 10.9 With text selected, click the Link icon to apply a hyperlink

You can add a link to any of the text on your page by highlighting it, then clicking on the **Link** icon in the window header.

A new window titled **Hyperlink** will open and allow you to add in the URL of the site or the page to which you want the highlighted text to link. To do this it is best to open the website or page you wish to link with and then copy this URL into the Hyperlink window in Blogger. It has to be letter perfect or you'll end up with a dead link.

Click on **OK** to complete the link. You'll now notice that the text you have highlighted will have been changed to hyperlinked text, underlined.

Finally, view your blog and check that the link works, directing you (or any of your visitors) to the chosen web page.

Blogger enhancements

To make your Blogger blog even more effective there are some useful tools that you can use.

- **Google Blog This:** Blogger was purchased by Google in 2003 and as part of their partnership there are some useful features to make blogging even easier. The Google toolbar, for example, has a feature 'Blog This'. Select this and if you have a Blogger account you can post your current link to your blog.

- **Blogger for Word:** There's also an intermittently available Blogger for Word tool that works with certain combinations of Word and Blogger, although updates to each application have led to compatibility problems.

- **Blogging on the go:** The best way to use Blogger is by logging on and entering your images and text. However, Blogger can also create posts automatically from e-mails. You must first enable this facility in the Settings section (click on the **Settings** tab and then **e-mail**). Enter a secret password (which prevents other mischievous potential contributors from posting on your site). The subject line of any e-mail you send becomes the title of the entry and the message text, the body text of that entry.

- **Advertising:** Popular websites make money by selling advertising space. If your blog is proving to be popular (or even modestly so) you can earn a little money by enrolling in the Google AdSense scheme. When you enrol in this, adverts are placed in your blog (and can be in almost any website) and enable text-based, photo or video adverts to be run from your blog. When people click on the ad they get taken to the advertiser's website and you get a small payment each time.

Promoting your blog

To drive visitors and readers to your blog you need to promote it. You can use the same techniques as are discussed later in Chapter 12 regarding your website, but here are a few additional techniques relating to your blog:

- **Informally:** First, and perhaps most obviously, the details of a family or group blog can be notified informally to family members of members of the relevant group. Mention the address in your communications, when you e-mail or even when you phone your relatives.

- **'E-mail this Post':** You can add this feature (again from the Settings tab in Blogger) to allow visitors to your blog to spread the word. This lets them e-mail their friends and colleagues with content from your blog by a simple click of a button.

- **Get Listed:** Blogger maintains a list of blogs that should be automatically updated when new blogs appear. Check that yours is there, by selecting the **Settings** tab then the option **Basic** and ensure that **Add your blog to our listings** is set to 'Yes'.

- **Link:** Blogs can be linked to websites and other blogs. Make use of this facility to connect to other blogs you like or which might have a similar readership. Ask the webmaster or blogger to consider a reciprocal link to your site.

Blogging etiquette

Finally a few words on etiquette. Etiquette is important on a blog. For some, the beauty of blogging – if not the Web in total – is that it is unregulated and, to a point, anarchic. But that does not give you free rein to say anything and everything. Nor should anyone who comments on your blog be allowed to be needlessly offensive. Remember that, even if someone sets up a blog anonymously, they can still be traced via their computer connection, so defamatory, insulting, racist or abusive comments can still be attributed.

As a host of a blog you will be expected to quickly remove anything of this nature that is posted to your blog in the form of visitor comments. You should also remove anything that looks suspicious or suggests a scam. Unfortunately scammers and others (generally termed the 'Web low life') don't miss an opportunity to catch out the unwary.

Wikis

Wikis are websites that feature a wide-ranging collection of web pages produced (generally) by a number of contributors. With a thorough regime of hyperlinks, a wiki can grow to form an encyclopaedic collection of articles and features that can form the premier web reference on certain subjects. Good examples are the iMDB movie database (that also covers television and video programming, actors and presenters) and, of course, Wikipedia. Wikipedia was not the archetype of the genre, but is certainly the best known.

The idea behind a wiki is that any contributor can edit a page or create new pages with just a conventional web browser. There is, of course, the risk that such a site – with unfettered access – could prove totally anarchic, so a typical wiki will include certain safeguards that can limit contributions and provide administrators and moderators with the means to control access and contributions.

Creating a wiki

In terms of the configuration, setting up a wiki is rather like setting up a blog. In the following example, I've used the online wiki creator Wetpaint, which you can find at **www.wetpaint.com**.

Step 1: Names and descriptions

You need first to create a name for your wiki. This should be something meaningful but if you subsequently think of a better name don't worry – you can change it later. You need also to provide a URL. In the same way that you might have done with Blogger, which appended '.blogspot.com' to your chosen name, this appends '.wetpaint.com'.

Figure 10.10 Wetpaint wiki: setting up a wiki is as easy as setting up a blog

Step 2: Explanatory notes

Now you can add a short explanation of what the wiki is about. This is a general description – but no more than a short paragraph. To emphasize or reinforce this description you can choose a category from the pull down menu to help visitors to find your site more easily.

Step 3: Determining who can contribute

The *raison d'être* of a wiki is that it thrives through collabora-
tion: it is a team effort rather than the work of an individual. As
such it can grow and develop fast, with experts on niche elements able to contribute their specialized knowledge. Though
anyone can normally read a wiki (though you can introduce limits
if you wish), you will need to determine who is allowed to contribute. The three options are:

- **Only people I invite:** use this if you only want contributions
  from a small controlled group. This is the best option if the
  wiki is designed for a closed group such as a club or association where contributions should be limited to members.

- **Anyone who joins the wiki:** this intermediate option requires
  that any contributor is welcome but that they must first join
  the wiki through a registration process. This ensures that
  contributors are accountable for any contributions that they
  make and that those contributions are attributable to them.

- **Everyone:** even anonymous contributions are welcome from
  anyone at all. This gives any wiki the best chance to grow
  and develop fast but there is always the risk of fatuous, irrelevant or absurd contributions, so the wiki needs to be carefully monitored to weed out any unsuitable material.

Step 4: Layout and design

Wetpaint provides an extensive range of options for the layout
and design of your wiki, based on simple templates. Choose one
that reflects its content and you will see a sample of the chosen
page displayed. If none of the templates is appropriate to your
subject you can upload an image or graphic to further customize
your production.

Step 5: Creating an account

Unless you've created something in Wetpaint before you can now
proceed to create an account. You'll probably know the form
here: you need to create a username, password and provide a
valid e-mail address along with some personal details (and note
that these do not display with your wiki).

Figure 10.11 Wetpaint provides a wide range of templates

Step 6: Invite some contributions

Like a conventional website or a blog, once you've created your wiki only you will be aware of it. Now, to get people to contribute you can invite them directly. Wetpaint provides the means at this stage: all you need do is enter the e-mail addresses of those people you wish to alert to the wiki and who might conceivably contribute.

Welcome! Wikis are websites that everyone can build together. It's easy! ⊗

EasyEdit ✐ ✐ Edit tags ✉ Email page ✔ Add a To-Do ✈ More tools (what's this?)

Team Members

*NOTE: If your group is posting names and phone numbers here, please go into your site's "Settings" and make the site **PRIVATE** so it cannot be viewed except by the invited members of your wiki.

Name	Email	Phone Number	Role
Joe Student	joe@college.edu	555-585-8888	

Wiki Tip:
To add more rows to a table, put your cursor in the last row of the table and right-click with your mouse. Select "Add row" from the tool tips menu.

See also: The Assignment | Project Schedule | Brainstorming | Rough Draft

Figure 10.12 Wetpaint also makes it easy to invite contributors and their contributions

You can also set these potential contributors up as one of three grades of contributor:

1 **Administrators:** can do anything – e.g. access site settings and controls, manage and modify pages, contribute, edit contributions, ban members or invite others.

2 **Moderators:** can use the editing tools, ban members or invite others to join.

3 **Registered users:** can edit pages, add images and participate in discussions.

If you want to create contributors at all three levels you'll need to send an e-mail to each group separately. You can also, if you merely want to set up a wiki at this point, skip this step.

Step 7: Start your wiki

Click on the 'Take me to my wiki' button to visit your wiki for the first time. A new wiki is a blank canvas – albeit on a template. You can, however, use the Site Wizard (which appears when you first open the wiki) to start populating it with some initial subpages as shown here.

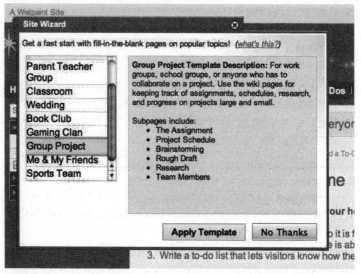

Figure 10.13 The Site Wizard lets you pre-populate your wiki with some standardized pages relevant to your subject

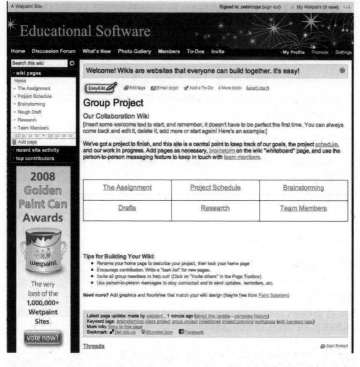

Figure 10.14 First page: now it's up to you and your contributors

Summary

You will have realized from this chapter that creating a blog or a wiki really is simple. However, you should also be aware that there are countless blogs on the Web and yours needs to be special in some way to stand out. Of course, some blogs such as family ones don't need or aim to be seen widely – they exist to service the needs and ambitions of a family. But if your intention is to be a fêted commentator on world events, you will need to work somewhat harder.

The good thing about blogging is that it is so easy to do that you can set up a blog just to practise your skills. Then, when you are sure you've something that will appeal to a wider audience you can start actively promoting yourself.

Wikis, by virtue of being a more recent addition to the Web scene, are thinner on the ground and so, if you have a good, credible idea for a venture, you stand a much better chance of starting and building a popular, successful site.

Remember too that both blogs and wikis, though stand-alone websites in their own right, can also be added as components of a conventional website.

> If you would like to learn more about blogging, look out for: **Teach Yourself Blogging** by Nat McBride and Jamie Cason.

11

producing a compelling site

In this chapter you will learn:

- how to produce compelling content for a website
- about important things to consider when producing content for other website types
- how to add a web photo gallery

Constructing a website can become a rather mechanical exercise. You can all too easily get embroiled in putting together the structural elements and design and forget the content. Sadly there are a great number of such sites on the Web; sites that started off with the most worthy of intentions but ended up, ultimately, as a prime example of style over substance. It's easy to get into this situation. Creating visually stunning websites can be absorbing and you can get drawn too deeply into the intriguing world of web design. Sadly, this can be to the detriment of your website's contents.

In this chapter I will take a break from the mechanics of website production and focus squarely on content. How do you generate that persuasive content that delivers a powerful website?

Family and genealogy websites

What's the difference between a family website and a genealogical one? The former tends to concentrate on the day-to-day life and experiences of a family – news, views and events – while the genealogical one is focused on the family through time, including long-departed members. The latter tends to be principally concerned with research – finding out more and more about the extended family. However, there can be significant overlaps between the two so it's best to consider them as one.

Interest in heritage and genealogy has skyrocketed in recent years and much of this can be attributed to the Web. The Web has made it simple to access vast annals of family documentation, whether personally promoted on the Web or delivered via national censuses and records. Websites such as Friends Reunited have spawned companion sites like Genes Reunited that use the power of the Web – and millions of subscribers – to create sophisticated extended family trees.

This top level co-ordination has not stopped individuals setting up – on behalf of their families – their own family trees, and using them as a hub for sharing all sorts of family information. The main reasons people set up their own site, then, are to:

• Discover, map and present genealogical information.

- Provide a central resource where family members can share their own information.

- An opportunity to archive images, photos and documents relating to family members past and present.

- Provide an information centre where family members can communicate, network and share information on events.

For many creators of these websites the most fascinating and compelling element is the ability to create a family tree, linking all the disparate members of the family that younger generations may only have heard of in passing.

Family trees

It would be simple to create a basic family tree using a drawing package and post this to a website, but why reinvent the wheel? Genealogical sites have certain layouts in common (family trees for example) that have already been produced by commercial and non-commercial website designers. Rather than starting from

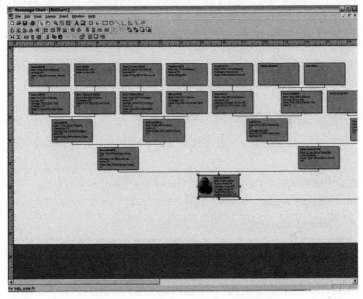

Figure 11.1 Genealogy software is adept at creating family trees that can then be pasted to websites

scratch, consider using one of these. It will save a great deal of time and most of these applications are better suited to an expanding tree. Remember, as your site gets more popular and more and more family members take a look, your family tree will inevitably grow!

For creating family trees, take a look at products such as Great Family (**www.greatprogs.com/greatfamily**) which is shareware. Other names to look out for are Reunion for Macintoshs (**www.leisterpro.com**) and Windows' RootsMagic (**www.rootsmagic.com**). All offer free trials.

Family histories

Family trees are great ways of pictorially representing a family but they are not suited to extended family histories. For these, it can be a good idea to link parts of your family tree to the pages of the family history.

Such histories need to be succinct (as always with web-based text) but also thoroughly researched. How might you go about this? Begin by noting down some key information that you are already familiar with. Put in the dates and names that immediately come to mind (if you have already compiled a family tree, then you could use this as the starting point). Include, for each family member:

- Birth date
- Date of death
- Age (yes, it can be calculated, but make it easy for your visitors!)
- Profession
- Place of birth
- Place of marriage
- Name of spouse(s)
- Children.

From this you can begin to establish links (valuable if you have not yet built a family tree) and note those members of your current family who could offer a greater insight.

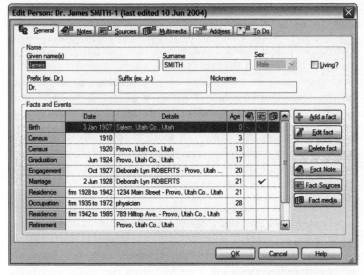

Figure 11.2 Genealogy software is also a great way for compiling and cross-referencing your research

Next, talk to relevant family members to extend this basic information. Be mindful that the memory of older members could be clouded by the passage of years. It can therefore be useful to talk to several members of the family about the same historical characters to get – as far as possible – an unbiased opinion.

Gather all the information together to form a definitive history, but do bear in mind that new information may come to light after you have finished. Indeed, if you've been going around asking for information, it could trigger memories that don't come to light straight away. Be prepared to update your history frequently (and this is the best part about family histories – they are never static).

Sharing memories

A family tree posted to a website can be, for all but the creator, a little dull. True, it's a way to discover your relationship to a long-forgotten second cousin, but beyond that it can be rather prosaic. The beauty of the Web is that you can enliven your site by making it an active forum where people can share information. They can, for example, provide photos of relatives so that you can, quite literally, put a face to a name.

The mechanics of doing this can vary according to the software used and the scale of the family. For a small, compact family the work may easily be undertaken by an individual, to whom relevant material can be e-mailed (or even physically posted) prior to being collected and placed on the website.

In larger families this can often work successfully as a collaborative venture, with more than one person – perhaps someone from each branch of the family – taking responsibility for posting the information and images.

It can be useful to provide a forum on the site so that still more family members can add information that you wouldn't necessarily want to append directly to the family tree, for example anecdotal stories. Forums can quickly grow in scope and range as stories and pictures jog long-forgotten memories and bring them to the fore.

Sharing news

Some family members – particularly the younger ones – are less focused on their family's past and can be a little reticent in visiting what they perceive to be a site all about dead people! To bring those of all ages to the site, many webmasters include a section dedicated to events, birthdays and current news. This becomes a useful place to visit to remember that birthday you always forget, to post information about a party or social occasion or even make birth or marriage announcements.

Finding information

As well as Genes Reunited (http://www.genesreunited.com) here are some other great sources of reference material for family histories and genealogical research:

- Ancestry.co.uk: **www.ancestry.co.uk**
- Find My Past: **www.findmypast.com**
- UK census information: **www.ukcensusonline.co.uk**

Check the costs when researching – not all information is free and you can rack up significant costs if retrieving a large amount of information or documentation.

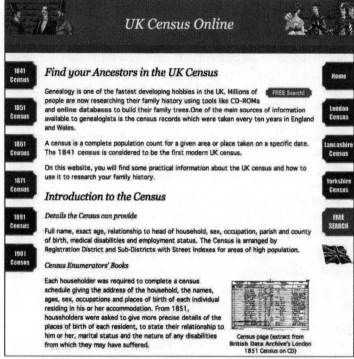

Figure 11.3 UK Census Online is great source of census information.

Photo gallery websites

Apart, perhaps, from blogs, photo galleries comprise the most numerous form of contemporary websites. We can put this down to two things. First, the huge popularity of digital cameras (whose images are easy to share in any digital medium). Second, the ease with which a photo gallery can be configured.

Photo finishers' photo gallery websites

Many photo processors, whose traditional business is processing films and producing prints for the customer, have diversified into online photo galleries that just about anyone can set up and upload images to. Of course there is an ulterior motive for this: the host will hope – if not expect – you to order prints from selected images. But the fact that the photo gallery is on the Web means anyone (or at least anyone you give access permissions to) can see the images and, should they choose, order prints.

Like all simple to use 'instant' websites, you suffer the constraints of having a limited range of display options and also a (deliberately) commercially-branded web address. It's best to think of these web galleries as a quick fix – if you want to share images quickly and give friends and relatives a chance to order prints (without the hassle of doing so yourself) then it's a good option.

Semi-bespoke web galleries

What if your photographic ambitions are loftier? Photo finishers' sites are great for the snap-shooter but don't smack of professionalism even if the images stored there are top notch.

Fortunately, there is an alternative that requires very little setting up in terms of configuring the gallery section and which can be uploaded to your web domain. These are the web galleries produced from image manipulation and editing applications.

The photographers' favourite application, Photoshop, and the enthusiast's version, Photoshop Elements, can both produce a gallery featuring your images and create all the requisite HTML. All you need do is upload one of them to your web space.

Here's how simple it is to create a web gallery using Photoshop Elements.

Step 1

Carefully select all the images that you want to use in your web photo gallery. Ruthlessly discard any that are below par in terms of composition, exposure or focus. Perform any edits on the images that might enhance them.

Step 2

Open Photoshop Elements (here I am using Photoshop Elements 6 for Windows – the commands will be slightly different for other versions) and select **Create** button **> Online Gallery**. A drag and drop panel entitled **Online Gallery** appears. (In Photoshop you would choose **File > Automate > Web Photo Gallery** to take you directly to the feature.)

Step 3

Drag and drop your images into the Online Gallery window. Click **Next** when you have completed your selection.

Step 4

Select a style template from the range provided. Use the pull-down menu to access alternative ranges of templates. Make sure that the style you choose is sympathetic to the images that you will be displaying in your gallery.

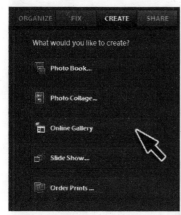

Figure 11.4 Photoshop Elements 6 – Web Photo Gallery

Figure 11.5 Photoshop Elements offers a wide range of gallery styles

Step 5

If you wish, add a title and subtitle. You can also add an e-mail address if you'd like this included in the gallery display. Click **Next** to move to the next stage.

Step 6

In Photoshop Elements the next stage lets you post your gallery to the Web in a number of different ways. I would suggest that before considering this you check the appearance of the gallery using web browsers. Test this as you would any other website.

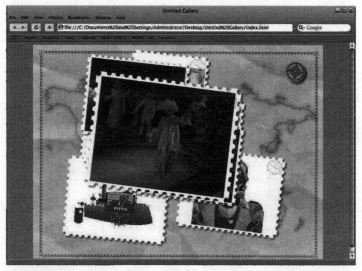

Figure 11.6 Check the appearance of any web gallery in a browser

The folder created contains three subfolders – images, thumbnails and pages. You can upload this to a website to act as a stand-alone web image gallery or add the folder (containing the subfolders) to a location on an existing website. Please bear in mind that the range of features and the precise step-by-step instructions will vary according to whether you use Photoshop or Photoshop Elements and which version of the application you have.

A semi-bespoke solution like this probably offers the best compromise between simplicity of construction and professionalism in the design. True, a Photoshop veteran will spot your design straightaway but for the majority of your visitors they will, if you have chosen well, just enjoy the photographs!

Fully bespoke solutions

Of course, if you don't want the Photoshop look you can opt for a fully bespoke website where you have ultimate control over the contents. This will let you determine:

- The entire design of your site.

- The size and quality of images used.

- The level of protection you want to provide (do you want people to download images unhindered or to you want to restrict them in some way?).

- The way your images are presented.

Of course, to get this right is more difficult than taking one of the off-the-shelf (or near off-the-shelf) solutions but if you want something that perfectly reflects the style you want to promote, it may be the only way forward.

I would suggest that if you are constructing your first site you start with the Photoshop-type option (other image editing applications provide similar routines) until you are comfortable with the ways you can present your images on screen. Websites do, after all, grow and evolve. Even the greatest and most popular of websites occasionally undertake a dramatic overhaul to take advantage of new technologies. You can do the same as your skills and knowledge of the Web grows.

Hobby and interest websites

In the website popularity stakes, after the family and photos come hobbies and special interests. The Web is, after all, the place where more and more people turn to first when researching information or when they want to discover more about their chosen interest. On the Web they can be almost assured of finding a site – or perhaps many sites – that cater for that interest.

Because people's hobbies and interests are so diverse, almost any format of website can be considered and, potentially, any template used. So you might choose a web gallery based format (or one that uses web galleries extensively) if your interest is something that demands good photos. That could range from cars, models or arts and crafts.

Some of these – such as arts and crafts and model making – may need strong supporting text, offering not only general information but also step-by-step projects or stage-by-stage illustrations of the progress of a project.

With such an open brief, how would you take your first steps? One way is to take a look at sites operated by others with a similar interest to your own. Then decide:

- Do you want to create a similar site? In which case, what will you do that is different, to make it worth visiting?

- Can you interpret your hobby or interest in quite a different, but better way?

You'll probably find, if you take a look at alternatives, that some will be rather old, at least in web design terms. They won't take advantage of today's easy and effective design tools. Use a more modern approach and you'll immediately score an advantage. Remember to think the same way as your visitors. This is easy if it's a shared interest or hobby. What would you like to see on the site? How would you like to see it presented? These are great starting points. Just remember, don't take too many good ideas from sites that could be similar to your own!

Information websites

Information websites were traditionally lumped together with hobby and interest sites in terms of their design and layout. They differed only in that the information content tended to be more wide-ranging than that of the hobby site. Such a site will also need to be designed with the topic and visitor profile in mind.

More recently we have seen that information site owners are increasingly adopting the wiki format. This meets the need of an information site well: it provides the scope to expand as required, allows multiple contributors and has a familiar but rigorously laid-out format.

Of course there is no need to follow the wiki format if you are planning an information-based site, but as a feature of your site it could be a convenient way for others to add their comments. You can, of course, edit and moderate any content supplied by others.

Figure 11.7 The hifi and tv enthusiast's website BeoWorld is full of technical information, product information, forums and more

Summary

So, for a good, well-rounded website you need more than good design or good content. You need both. The best way to assess your site, whether at the planning stage or during building, is to put yourself in the position of a visitor. Imagine (and it's not too hard as you will have been a visitor to other sites) what they will want to see and what they might like to see. Think too what irritates you when visiting other sites. Make sure you don't make the same mistakes!

12

promoting your website

In this chapter you will learn:

- how to appear on a search engine
- how you can optimize the use of a search engine
- how to use reciprocal linking
- ways to may your site 'sticky'

Once your website is up on the Web it's there for anyone to visit. But, and it's that proverbial big 'but', you won't find yourself overrun with visitors. Indeed, you may not have any. That's a bit disappointing considering all the work you have put into creating your site. There is worse to come. Enter some keywords relating to your newly launched website into Google or some other search engine and there will be no sign of it.

Websites and search engines

So what's gone wrong? Actually, nothing. For a start, your website is new and you're unlikely to get any visitors until people know about it. The way that potential visitors will get to know about your site is likely to be via a search engine. So why can't a search engine find you? Because it too, has yet to discover you. To understand this better you need to know the mechanism that search engines use to deliver lists of potentially interesting sites to inquisitive surfers.

Indexing

Consider this analogy. Imagine you and your friends have been collaborating on a large reference book. Each of you writes a distinct section and, periodically, all these are gathered together in a ring binder. Periodically one of your collaborators comes along and creates an index. Then you all add some more material.

Now imagine someone comes along to use this reference book. They can look up, in the index, content that interests them. However, because this is an ongoing project, they won't be able to use the index to find pages that have been added since the last index was compiled.

This is pretty much the way the Web works. The sections you and your friends write can be compared to websites; the index to the search engine. When your website goes live you could try using a search engine to find it – as any potential visitors might – but will probably be disappointed. Basically, the search engine needs to detect and index your website before it can include it as a search result. As you can probably imagine, indexing the whole of the Web is a big task even for powerful indexing programs. So your site may not appear in a search engine for a few hours, a few days or perhaps as long as a few months.

Even when your site does appear in a search engine's listing it may not do so in the way that you expect. Some of the words and terms that you might expect visitors to use to search for your site may not correlate with those used by the search engine. So, to get the best possible success and to increase the chance of visitors seeing your website as swiftly and precisely as you wish, you need to optimize your site. This is a process called search engine optimization.

Figure 12.1 Search engines are not all alike in the way that they retrieve and deliver information but use similar processes for searching. This is newcomer Cuil

Search engine optimization

Search engine optimization is the process of improving the number of hits on a website and, perhaps more significantly, the quality of those hits from visitors who use search engines. This can involve modifying your site directly (so it is more easily and effectively handled by search engines) or submitting your site – manually or automatically – to specific search engines.

When a potential visitor to your site enters a keyword or phrase into the search box of, say, Google, a list of websites that correspond with that phrase is returned. Notionally you would expect those sites whose names or details include the exact phrase to be listed at the top and those that less closely match the phrase (perhaps including all the words, but not necessarily in the same order) to appear lower.

If you want your website to receive good exposure in search engines you need first to think in the way that those potential visitors do. When you use a search engine to find some information, what do you do with the list of matching sites? You tend to look at the first half dozen or so and click on them first. Only if these don't deliver the information you need do you work your way further through the list.

In practice you are very unlikely to get your site listed highly by a search engine if the description given by a visitor is broad in its scope. For example, if your site is about modelling aircraft, the top entries in any search engine are likely to be taken by either those (normally commercial) sites that have paid for the privilege or those very precisely optimized. However, if your site is specifically devoted to modelling Second World War Catalinas, and a visitor enters these more precise terms, you are more likely to feature higher up the list.

Search engines employ techniques that involve trawling the Web, recording and indexing information on websites. To get good visibility – indeed, to get visibility at all – you need to ensure that the programs that scan the Internet (called crawlers and spiders) can see applicable information on your site.

Increasing visibility

So, how can you ensure that your site receives the best possible visibility? If money is no object (and for some of the largest commercial sites it isn't) you can work with an agency devoted to Web placements. They will ensure that your site gains a lofty position in any searches. This can be costly – very costly – as these agencies often charge per click. Every time a visitor clicks on a search engine link to your site, you pay a fee. For commercial sites, and particularly sites that operate site-based shops, this is of little consequence. If a good proportion of those clicks result in purchases from the site then the more clicks the better. For a non-commercial site, heavy traffic (in the form of many clicks) would be welcome, paying for each would be less so.

Agencies will use an alternative technique that will also serve your site well. It involves optimizing the content of your website so that the web crawlers can better latch on as they trawl their way through. The easiest way to ensure at least some exposure involves putting the key objectives, aims and subject of your website on the home page. Include all the principal subjects covered and also, for good measure, include the name of the website itself. You would probably find that you did this as a matter of course in the introductory text on your home page.

Submitting your site to a search engine

When it comes to collecting visitors, the search engine will need to be a well respected friend. But that friendship and respect needs to be earned. Increasing your chance of being picked up by a web crawler is a bit like raising your hand in a crowd. You'll be seen if yours is the only hand raised, but if most of the other people there have their hands raised too, it would take an observer (the equivalent to a web crawler) a long time to identify everyone. So it is on the Web. Careful wording and crafting has made you more visible, but if similar actions by other site owners raise their visibility too it can take some time for your site to be recognized and listed.

You can speed up the process by submitting your site to a site engine yourself. Here's how. For this example, due only to its market share, I have chosen to use Google. Because it is so popular it makes a good place to start, but subsequently you may choose to replicate this action with different lists of search engines, particularly if some engines are better suited to websites that are similar to yours.

Step 1

At Google (**www.google.co.uk** or **www.google.com**) click on the **About Google** link in the homepage window.

Figure 12.2 Google's homepage: the About Google link is indicated

Step 2

The About Google window has many options. Locate and click on the **Add your site** option.

Step 3

Enter the URL of your site. This is the full name of your site that appears in the browser's window. Note that it asks for the full URL: this means that you need to include the prefix http://, not just the section of the address more commonly quoted, that usually begins with the 'www'.

Step 4

In the comments section add a few succinct words that would help people to find your site, and which give crucial information about it. Brevity is the key here. 'A site for Catalina aircraft modellers' or 'Modelling of Catalina aircraft' in the case of the example mentioned earlier.

Figure 12.3 Locate the 'Add your site' option

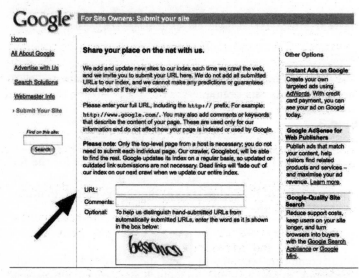

Figure 12.4 Enter your full URL, beginning with the HTTP://

Step 5

Click on the **Add URL** button to submit your details. Resist the urge to use Google to find your site immediately. Unless your site has been up and running for some time and Google's web crawlers have found it, it will take a little time for it to be listed.

Optimizing HTML for search engines

You can also (instead of or, better, in addition to the steps described above) modify the HTML of your website to make search engines better recognize and interpret your site's content. If you're quite happy to avoid any HTML programming let me allay any concerns: the modifications needed to the HTML are no more complex than typing in a paragraph on a word processor.

No matter how you produce your website, when it goes live (on the Web or even on your computer) all the layouts, the text and just about every other aspect of the site is represented in HTML. You can display the HTML by using the **View Source** command. This is called the **Page Source** command in Firefox. In either case, you'll normally find the option in the **View** menu.

When you select this command you'll see the HTML coding for the site. Pay particular attention to the section, near the top comprising a title and comments, often prefixed by <! to indicate a comment (that is, text to be read but not part of the programming content of the page). You'll find here descriptions of the site that you won't necessarily see in the visible wording on the site. This is the text prepared for the search engines to see and use to identify your site.

You can use the HTML feature in your web authoring application to add something pertinent. For the modelling example you might put:

```
<!-Catalinamodelling is the only site devoted
to modelling and building replicas of the
Catalina flying boat. We welcome contributions
by anyone interested in this flying boat or
aircraft and airplanes -!>
```

Because this text will effectively be ignored in producing your website (as it is identified as comment text) it could be placed anywhere in the HTML code but it is best placed near the top, below the title text, which is written between the HTML tags <title> and </title>.

Use and abuse of meta tags

Meta tags are special lines of HTML code that also appear in the top, header section of an HTML page. These lines contain text that, like the comments, doesn't appear on screen but is seen by search engines. HTML programmers will include two meta tag lines, called meta keywords and meta description.

In meta keywords will go all the keywords relating to the site. In the meta description field will go a full and proper description of the site, perhaps replicating that in the comment field I described earlier.

You do not have to include meta tag lines in your code, but doing so does increase your site visibility. That may be just a little but, in concert with the other ways you use, it gives your site an advantage. The disappointing thing is that because the principal reason for using these meta tags is to give your site visibility, many website owners pack them full of keywords that have only a remote connection with the subject of the site, hoping that this will broaden the site's ability to be listed. This misuse has meant that some search engines now ignore meta tag lines. The search engine business is competitive and the company behind each engine wants to ensure that visitors return to them because they deliver the best links.

Exploiting links

Because of the abuse of meta tags, the way your site uses links can now be considered more important with regard to search engine performance. It is the links that you provide between pages – and most significantly, from the superficial home and linking pages to the serious content of the site – that the web crawlers and web spiders use to produce their indexes. So it is important – vitally important – that the links between pages are sound. Otherwise there's a very real risk that great swathes of your site are not visible to be indexed and will be ignored.

Of equal significance are external links, links from one website to another. As I've said before, if a great number of websites link to yours then it will be assumed that your site is significant and worthy of a higher ranking. But there tends to be something of a hierarchy here. Yes, being linked from a number of other sites will confer a higher ranking, but the ranking of those other sites will have a bearing on how high your ranking is: if the other sites are highly ranked, that will give you an even higher ranking than if your site was linked from a similar number of more lowly sites.

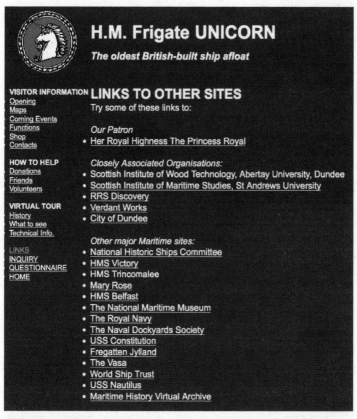

Figure 12.5 Links on a website don't just provide useful connections, they improve your website's visibility

It pays, then, as part of your promotional activities, to get linked to as many sites as possible. Most websites are only too happy to include a section of links to other sites on the basis that in doing so they will equally get a reciprocal link from many of these sites too. You can set about linking to other sites by typing your site's keywords into a search engine and looking at the listing returned. You could contact these sites (or, rather their webmasters) and request inclusion in their list of links on the promise of doing so yourself, though often this doesn't solicit a response. Better to include links yourself. Others will soon reciprocate.

Soon, if your site is up to scratch, you'll find your site listed as a link on other sites. Don't worry that you are new to the business, unless the webmaster determines that a link to your site is inappropriate, a link to a new site still adds to the tally of links and if your site grows in stature (both in terms of its content and its search engine listing) it can only serve linked sites well.

The only exception to this sharing scheme, if your site is of a commercial nature, will be those of competitors. Although applying to them will be a waste of time, be aware of them and, more particularly, of the links listed on their site. The linked sites could be approached with a view to adding to your raft.

Use **View Source** or its equivalent in other browsers to reveal the source HTML code of a web page. You can see what wording others use to define their sites and make them more responsive to search engines.

More search engine tips

To further exploit search engines you need to take every opportunity to give your site, in visibility terms, the edge. Here are a few more tips to help you achieve that:

+ Add **ALT** text to your images: A few chapters ago, when we discussed the use of images on websites, I mentioned ALT text. This, as you may recall, was text added to describe an image so that those that could not see your website (or cannot see graphics and images displayed) can understand what should be displayed. As well as improving the accessibility of your site, ALT text provides search engines with an extra way of indexing your site.

♦ Write good, meaningful copy: Not only does a website benefit from short, punchy editorial text on each page, but that text must contain all the keywords that potential visitors may choose when looking for your site.

♦ Check your links: It's easy, as your site grows and develops, for carefully crafted hyperlinks between pages to become broken. This can be irritating for visitors.

♦ Make best use of keywords by using 'nested keywords' or keywords that contain other keywords. Using extended words such as 'modelling' will generate hits from people searching using both 'model' and 'modelling' as their keyword.

♦ Arrange keywords in a sequence based on the way people are likely to use them – this will ensure that the search engine lists your site higher than another that uses the words in a more random order.

♦ Ensure that the most significant keywords are in the HTML title tag of each page. If possible (without affecting the text

---

Google General FAQ

Frequently Asked Questions

Find more answers and discuss Google services in our **user support discussion forum**.

- **Search Questions**
    1. Why am I suddenly seeing pop-up ads on Google?
    2. How do I narrow my search?
    3. How can I restrict my search?
    4. How do I stop my previous searches from appearing when I type in a new search term?
    5. How can I set the default number of hits to 100?
    6. How are query results listed?
- **International Questions**
    1. How can I get back to the Google homepage in English?
    2. Why is Google displaying in another language when I didn't set any language preferences?
    3. How can I improve the accuracy or number of results when searching for foreign words?
    4. Why does Google not offer more language choices?
    5. How do I suggest a translation or spelling improvement?

My question is not answered here. Where can I send my question?

Figure 12.6 Google Frequently Asked Questions is a good place to improve your search ranking

flow) repeat these words in the body text of each page as close to the top as possible.

♦ Search engines focus on significant words and especially nouns and verbs. Other parts of speech such as pronouns, prepositions and articles are generally not included.

Bear in mind that search engines feature comprehensive advice and FAQs on placement and rankings, and these can also help you discover why, for example, one site ranks you in a different manner from another.

Keeping hold of your visitors

Reciprocal links with other sites that share your potential interest groups is a great way to direct visitors to your site, albeit with the minor caveat that your links to other sites will occasionally take a few away. What else can you do to publicize your site and drive visitors to you? More to the point, once you get visitors on your site you need to keep them there. If your site contains some especially compelling content then you may need to do little – people will return as a matter of course. But, I suspect, few sites will be so compelling, and even the best of these will eventually risk losing their magic attraction.

To ensure that you retain as many visitors as possible and keep them coming back, you need to make your site, 'sticky'. A sticky website is one that has visitors coming back time and time again or, when they do visit, staying there for longer.

Here are some tools that webmasters use to keep visitors longer and get them to return.

Refreshed content

Why do most visitors come back to a website? They come, in the first place, for good content, but then for content that is refreshed on a regular basis – so there is always something new to see. That doesn't necessarily mean that you throw out old material. There will always be potential new visitors who will want to see your original content and some repeat visitors may value older material. New content should appear first on the home page – where it is more visible and more likely to make an impression on any visitors.

Blogs

By their very nature, blogs are diaries designed to have new content added regularly. As well as stand-alone blog-based websites, you can add a blog as part of any site. Adding a blog, per se, will not make your site stickier – the contents of that blog needs to attract people. Once you've started to hook people by virtue of a blog you need to add content regularly. Visitors hooked by your blog will soon desert you if they come to read your latest entries and find nothing's been added for a while.

Forums, chat rooms

Enthusiasts like to exchange views with like-minded peers. So, adding a forum or chat room to your site can make it a destination for enthusiasts to share their thoughts and ideas. This method scores in two ways – the content of your site is refreshed regularly (very regularly if the forums become popular) and that refreshed content is provided by others.

The only downside to a forum or chat room is that you will need to ensure they are properly monitored or moderated so that content that may be offensive or wildly off topic (and therefore likely to dilute the focus of the site) can be quickly removed.

Adding content to social networking sites

Social networking sites such as Facebook allow people to collect and share useful information amongst their friends and colleagues on the site. You can make it simple for people to do so by adding buttons to your website that will post articles, features or images to the reader's page on the social networking site. You can see these buttons increasingly on websites especially those that provide news and views.

Many website authoring applications include the tools to add these 'share' buttons, but you can also visit the respective networking sites to get more information on linking to each.

> MORE NEWS

Figure 12.7 Many news and information sites include buttons to link to social networking sites

Links

I have already discussed the practical use of links to other websites for enhancing search engine listing, but those links are also great for getting people to your site. That way, you trade on the popularity of other sites that are – in some way – connected to your own. The payback is that as your popularity grows the links from your site will be used by visitors to explore further. But, if your site is popular enough to have a raft of visitors, they are likely to return in any case – so long as the content is up to the mark!

Conventional offline promotions

Don't forget or underestimate the power of more conventional promotional techniques. Adding the URL of your website to your e-mail signature, in flyers and even magazines can alert potential visitors to your website. Some of these suggestions might appear low tech but can help you get to potential visitors that you might not otherwise address.

Take care in some promotions: for example, outright advertising of your website on another site's forum or chat room is generally frowned upon.

Measuring your website traffic

How do you determine how successful you have been in promoting your website? In terms of search engine performance the ranking you achieve is an instant indicator. However, determining how sticky your website is can be less obvious. To understand the stickiness of your site you need to know:

- How many visitors you have to your site.

- How many of those visitors are returning.

- The number of referrals to your site from search engines.

- The number of referrals to your site from other sites.

- The number (or percentage) of visitors who bookmark your site.

These statistics – and a great deal more – can be accessed using a web statistics package. Basic packages for generating statistics are available on the Web and can be found by using your favourite search engine. More complex and thorough analytical packages are also available, but these tend to be commercially focused and you'll have to pay to use them. This is also on the basis that the more detailed (and, potentially, meaningful) the statistics are the more you'll pay.

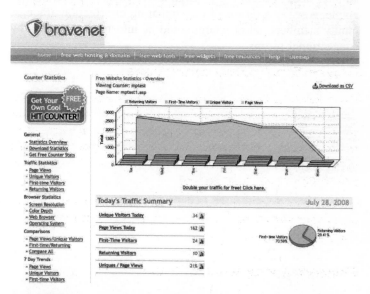

Figure 12.8 Bravenet is a convenient source of many website plug-ins – this example gives very detailed information on visitors

You will need to assess whether these provide good value for money, and that will depend very much on the nature of your website. If your website is operated as a hobby, or to present information about your hobby, paying for detailed statistics may be neither viable nor affordable. However, if your site is – or features – an online store, you may want to know a lot of details about visitors and their habits. In this case, costs are often justifiable as they can help deliver greater sales.

Summary

You will have recognized by that creating a compelling site is by no means a guarantee of achieving popularity. To gain visibility you'll also need to ensure that you take some action to promote yourself with regard to search engines and more generally. True, some visibility will be achieved by doing nothing – web crawlers and spiders will eventually detect and index your site and this may be sufficient for your needs. Do be aware though that not all sites need widespread promotion: a family website, for example, is really a means of disseminating information amongst family members, all of whom could be informed of the site by conventional means.

13

making money from your website

In this chapter you will learn:

- about ways of earning money from your website
- how to add a store to your site
- how to create a web store

Today, just about everyone is used to buying goods or services on the Internet. Sites like Amazon and eBay have made surfing and shopping a pastime for some and an obsession for others. There are many reasons why people use the Internet to shop. Some find it more convenient than making a trip to the nearest shopping centre. Others find it the way of purchasing specialized items that you'd be unlikely to find anywhere else. And, of course, there will be those who want to seek out a bargain.

Why sell on the Web?

For sites like Amazon, selling is the sole reason for their website. Though you might visit to window-shop – or perhaps get news and opinion on selected books and DVDs – Amazon, like its peers, expects that you will eventually purchase something. Other websites are not principally focused on selling but may provide a web shop as an additional feature. Examples include those hobby or activity sites that sell books and resources relevant to eager visitors.

It is perhaps obvious that most people set about selling anything in order to earn money. Those set up on the Web are no different. For some the whole purpose of setting up a website is to create an online shop, for others it's to raise a little money, perhaps just sufficient to fund the site. There are many ways you can sell, or make money, using your website, and in this chapter I'll guide you through the most significant.

Passive selling

The easiest way to make a modest amount of money from your website is to do so passively. No need to worry about payment management, payment security, maintaining a shop or any stock inventory. Passive selling involves placing sales tools on your web pages, sales tools that will earn you money. What do I mean by sales tools? These are mostly hyperlinked adverts. Every time someone visits your website and then clicks on one of these ads, they get taken to the advertiser's website. In exchange for providing this link you get a small payment – a small commission, if you like – from the advertiser.

The amount you'll earn from these so-called click-throughs is small and the actual amount depends mainly on the site's popularity. Potential advertisers will clamour to have their ads placed on popular websites that can guarantee either a large number of visitors or a good number of visitors that meet the profile of the likely customer of the advertiser's product.

If you are lucky – and the owner of a popular website – you can score twice for advert placement. You can get a fee for having the advert placed on the site and a payment for the click-throughs. Depending on the product, you may even get a payment when a customer eventually purchases it.

Passive selling with AdSense

We are, perhaps, getting a little ahead of ourselves here. To reach this level of advertising success you need to have a popular site that can guarantee a certain level of visitors. And you'll need to conclusively prove the number and profile of your visitors.

In the meantime, as your site is young and developing, only beginning to gather a loyal following, is there any advertising that you can earn money from? Of course, the answer is 'yes'.

The easiest is to use Google AdSense. This scheme, which I mentioned briefly in regard to blogging, can be used to place ads in just about any website and, better still, the ads can be matched to the content of the site. That means you can select the type of advertiser and customize the ads so that the colour scheme used matches that of your site. That's particularly useful when you've spent a lot of time and much effort getting your site looking perfect.

The process of adding these advertisements is, you'll be pleased to hear, very straightforward. You need first to apply to Google (visit **www.google.co.uk/adsense**) and, once your application is accepted, you'll be given an account. Then you can customize the space available on your web page for the placement of ads, copy and paste in a block of HTML, and that's it. You even get full instructions along the way.

You have pretty much full control over the content so you can, for example, filter out ads from specific advertisers (essential if

Earn money from relevant ads on your website

Google AdSense matches ads to your site's content, and you earn money whenever your visitors click on them.

Figure 13.1 Google AdSense is a quick way to get relevant paid-for ads on your website

there are any ethical issues that prevent you screening certain ads) or others, say, from competitors (equally essential if your site is competing for visitors with another).

How do you get paid? Every time anyone clicks on an AdSense ad on your website you get credited. The more visitors you get who click on the ads, the more you'll get. If your site is gaining popularity, advertisers (or potential advertisers) can bid to appear on your site. You will then get paid on a monthly basis according to the balance of your account.

Google don't publish the amount you'll get paid because it does vary so much. Each click can earn a small fraction of a penny through to something much more substantial, depending on the site, the advertiser and the popularity. Google recommend you sign up and monitor your account to get an accurate idea of your income and, unfortunately for those wanting to predict the opportunities, that is the best way.

Third-party web stores

Something of a diversion this, and I won't labour too long on it as it does not involve developing your own web store. Working with a third party means that you don't develop a full web store but instead you produce essentially a department within a well known existing brand.

These stores provide a great way of getting into e-commerce without the need to develop everything – from sales and marketing strategies through building the shop and arranging payment systems – yourself. People in search of the products that you offer will often take a look at Amazon and eBay as a matter of course and so you (or, rather, your products) will have a level of visibility that it would take some time to develop were you to start a new store from scratch.

When you start a shop on eBay you would probably adopt the Shop Inventory format. Unlike the auction format sales by which eBay developed its reputation, these are Buy-it-Now format sales

Grow Your Sales with eBay Shops!

Subscribe now for as little as £6.00 a month.

Open a Shop

Maximise your success on eBay
with eBay Shops –
the leading, comprehensive e-commerce solution

75% of eBay Shops sellers surveyed said that opening an eBay Shop increased their sales.**

Get more from eBay's access to over 180 million shoppers worldwide.

* Showcase all your listings in your own customisable eBay storefront
* Build your brand in minutes with our Quick Shop Set-up
* Boost sales with marketing tools that keep buyers coming back
* Economically list for longer durations with Shop Inventory

Get more from eBay's access to over 180 million shoppers worldwide.

* Showcase all your listings in your own customisable eBay storefront
* Build your brand in minutes with our Quick Shop Set-up
* Boost sales with marketing tools that keep buyers coming back
* Economically list for longer durations with Shop Inventory

Figure 13.2 Shops on eBay: some retailers cover all options by including a store on eBay

that are listed for short or extended periods. Items can be bought using eBay's own PayPal system (fast and secure, but comparatively expensive) or you can opt for more conventional forms of payment. If you anticipate a large turnover, then you can sign up with an organization such as WorldPay (**www.WorldPay.com**) or Verisign (**www.verisign.com**) to accept credit/debit card transactions.

It's worth noting that, because shoppers tend to visit sites like eBay regularly, many companies that offer conventional web based stores also have a presence there. That way they keep all their options open and can be better placed to win sales no matter what route the shoppers take. If you decide that a web store is for you, then you too may consider having a second branch on eBay. The eBay Help system gives you full information on setting up a shop at their site.

Your own web shop

Before you consider whether or not to set up your own web shop, you need to consider what it is you intend to sell. Ask yourself some questions:

- Is you product something that will sell well through a website and a web store?

- Is it something that is more keenly priced than it would be on the high street?

- Do other websites stock it? And at what price?

- Are the prospective purchasers likely to shop online?

- Is it available at all on the high street?

- Can you post it easily and safely?

- Can you handle the logistics (getting the stock, packaging it and despatching)?

- Is there a real, untapped market for the product?

- Will your store get the visibility necessary to attract potential purchasers?

Researching your market

Getting a new bricks-and-mortar store involves a serious investment in cash and a detailed business plan if there is going to be
any chance of success. Even so, and despite hard work by all
concerned, many new stores fail. The Web is no different. There
is no physical store to worry about (or the consequent costs),
but that does not make the job of creating a successful venture
any easier. A store on the high street will get exposure and visitors just from people walking by; without careful marketing your
web store may not get any serious exposure. It will be an uphill
battle starting a store from scratch.

Many of the more successful sales operations (to distinguish them
from web stores) tend to get born from an existing popular
website. There is the realization from the webmaster that the
website has a loyal following and has become something of a
brand itself. People enjoy visiting and enjoy being associated
with it. That is sufficient to spur on a sales arm that sells products closely related to the site and even sharing the same brand-
ing. From that, the sales catalogue can grow to include those
products that share a common link.

Whatever your motivation to set up an online sales operation,
do make sure you research thoroughly. Returning to the list of
questions above, simply asking yourself, or trusted friends or
colleagues, can alert you to any problems. You may find that the
Web is awash with similar products at a fraction of the price. Or
that the typical shopper for them is unlikely to have a computer,
let alone Internet connectivity. And, practically, those low-cost
glass chandeliers you've cornered the market in need to be delivered personally rather than being consigned to the post – not a
viable option at all.

A simple web shop

Let me assume you've done your homework, discovered there is
a market for your product or service and you have sufficient
web presence to justify it. What should be your next step? There
are three main ways that you can start developing your embryonic store. At the top of the tree is to produce a fully bespoke
store, written by you (or for you) and designed precisely for

your product range and your way of selling. Then, occupying the middle ground, are the stores produced by using web shop authoring packages. These packages (which are often included as part of website authoring applications, including some of the later versions of WebPlus) work in a similar way to those packages but have an emphasis on the creation of store elements. I will take a look at these shortly.

The simplest solution and arguably the best for someone taking their first steps on the path to e-commerce is to use an online web shop that you can configure to your exact needs through your web browser. I use the word 'exact' here rather cautiously, as one of the limitations is that this option is often very restricted in the amount of customization possible. Rather than creating a shop from scratch or from templates, you 'rent' store space and that space is governed by the number of items that you want to sell. The cost will also vary according to the number of visitors you have to the shop and the number of items for sale.

You'll pay more if you want to sell more products (naturally) but, as you go up the cost scale, not only will you have more flexibility you will often have access to more features such as searchable catalogues of products – particularly useful if you have or plan an extensive inventory.

Pros and cons of a rented site

The key advantage of this approach is that you will have all the payment side taken care of automatically and – of particular importance to visitors – securely. Shoppers who purchase will normally be able to pay using PayPal or an alternative such as WorldPay. Also, because you create and manage the site through a browser, you can modify or update the site from any computer, rather than just the one upon which you originally built the site.

Another pro is that these hosted web shops spend a lot of time making themselves search engine friendly so that your store stands a good chance of getting seen and being well served by search engines.

Pouchee Purse Organizer

Haute Purse Couture

ADPRO Sports

Squishi Clothing

Figure 13.3 An automated shopping cart: sites like Shopify let you get going with a simple web shop fast

The drawback is that these stores are rather rigorous in the way they deliver the site layout for you. If you are linking this shop to your own, main, website you'll undoubtedly find it has a quite different design and style of operation. This solution is also not necessarily open-ended. Though you may be able to build a moderately extensive shop, you may eventually outgrow it. At that point you'll have no alternative but to transfer your store to a new system.

Some, but not all, hosted web stores can integrate with an existing website. A good example of a rented, hosted site is EKM Powershop (**www.ekmpowershop.com**), shown in Figure 13.4.

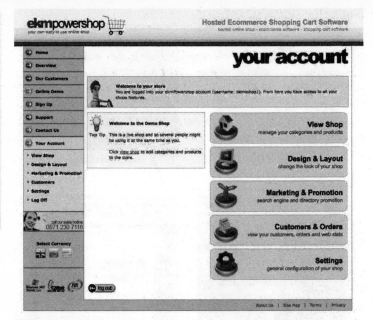

Figure 13.4 EKM Powershop is a good example of a hosted web store

A customized web shop

If you have used a typical web authoring package to create your main website you'll have no trouble adding a web shop to it – or creating a stand-alone store – using the similar tools provided by web shop creation software. These solutions use templates (usually with a much more comprehensive selection than offered by hosting companies) and wizards to guide you through the complete process prior to generating all the HTML that you will need to launch your site. You can even add snippets of HTML to modify the original code to offer specific additional features, again as you might with your website.

These are a good choice if you need a shop that is more sophisticated than the simple automated solutions discussed in the previous section and you are willing to devote a little more time to the project. Though a store like this is relatively easy to construct, you will have the additional hassle (modest though it may be) of also setting yourself up to accept automated payments. This might be using PayPal, WorldPay or Verisign.

Security considerations

An increasingly important consideration for any shop is security. Your potential customers will be justifiably concerned that, if they trust you with any financial information or payment, it will be correctly handled. There are plenty of tales of abuse on the Web, many of which are more apocryphal than real but, all the same, trust on the Web is very important. Of course, if you are just setting up in business you'll have to expect your customers to trust you as you will have no track record.

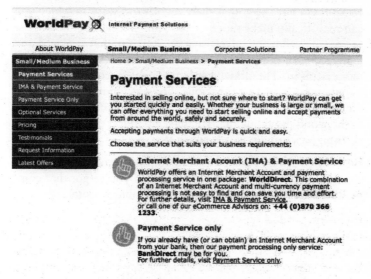

Figure 13.5 Having an organization such as WorldPay handle your transactions gives your purchasers confidence and avoids the need to employ the ultimate security systems

You can achieve a good degree of trust by using a proven mechanism (such as PayPal or WorldPay) to handle transactions, but you should also ensure that your site or payment handling system operates at the highest level of security. In most cases you can often entrust this to your payment company. You may have seen – if you've ever purchased from a modest online store rather than one of the online retailing giants – that, after confirming your purchases and prior to submitting any personal details, you get transferred to, say, WorldPay, to enter this information. This site and its peers operate the highest level of security so, as a customer, you can be assured of the most secure service.

As a store owner or manager this system works in your favour and provides you with the assurance that secure systems are being used for your transactions without you needing to invoke high levels of security directly on your website.

Summary

So you will have seen that there are several ways in which you can realistically make money from your website. Some of these are passive: allowing advertising on your site that is placed and managed by a third party. You can just sit back and watch the money roll in. The drawback is that, unless your site is really popular and visited by rapacious shoppers, your income will be modest. However, on the basis that you would otherwise receive nothing and providing that you have no moral objections to advertising, it's usually worth giving it a go.

Web stores demand more work to configure and more ongoing work to service the sales, but they can, if you've got that competitive edge, provide you with a more robust income.

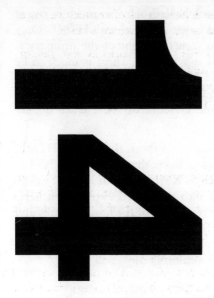

14

web design from scratch

In this chapter you will learn:

- some basic aspects of HTML
- how an HTML page is structured
- about stylesheets

Website authoring applications have evolved so much in recent years that there is little need to get involved with HTML. Only when we might want to do something out of the ordinary is there a need to delve, albeit superficially. There is much to be said for this ability to avoid HTML. If everyone who wanted any sort of web presence could only achieve their aims only by using HTML, the Web would undoubtedly be a much quieter place than it is today.

In this chapter we will dip our metaphorical toes into HTML. There are so many books and websites that specialize in HTML (and its spiritual siblings such as XML, XHTML) that it would be inappropriate to launch into a detailed exploration here. However, it is worth discovering a few of the basic features and concepts, as a basic knowledge can enhance your understanding of how websites work and, ultimately, allow you to personalize a website beyond what your authoring tools will permit.

The basics of HTML

Although it looks very much like one, HTML is not a computer programming language. Rather, it's a sequence of instructions that are given to a web browser in order to determine the layout of pages. Unlike a computer program which can fail if there is the smallest error in the syntax, HTML is much more tolerant. Even with a few significant gaffs you will still be able to display a web page – even though it may not appear as you intended. It's therefore easy to learn your way around without the disheartening failures that plague the novice computer programmer taking his or her first steps in C or some other high level language.

Creating a page of HTML

You create a page of HTML using a series of commands, or 'tags', which contain the HTML instructions to the web browser. Tags are placed at either end of the item that they apply to. An opening tag precedes the item and (usually, but not always) a closing one follows it. The closing tag is the same as the opening tag but has a / before the tag name. The whole tag in each case is enclosed in angle brackets (< and >).

For example, the HTML tag for representing text as italics is
<em>. To represent a word or phrase on the page in italics you
would enclose it with an opening or closing italics tag:

```
<em> Italicised Text </em>
```

HTML tags define the appearance of text on the page. What if
you want to add an image? You use an image source tag (which
links to an image and places it at the respective position):

```
<img src='image name.jpg'>
```

To be displayed, the image 'image name.jpg' needs to be uploaded
to, and stored with, other components of the web page.

Here are some examples of HTML tags:

<em>	italicized text
<strong> or <b>	bold text
<u>	underlined text
<font size=n>	font size (n is an integer)
<font face='name'>	font for text (e.g. 'Arial' or 'Tahoma')
<bgcolor='ffffff'>	colour (of background)
<p>	new paragraph
 	line break

You can combine tags. So, for example, you can specify a font
size, colour and that you want it bold, by consecutive use of
tags.

```
<font size=2 color='00ff00'><b>bold, coloured,
text</b></font>
```

HTML page structure

A typical page of HTML (which you can view for any page by
choosing **View Source** in your browser) has the structure:

```
<HTML>
<head>
<title>Web Page Title</title>
</head>
```

```
<body>
The content of the page – text, images, movies, etc
</body>
</HTML>
```

This first instructs the browser that what follows is HTML. The head information features items that do not normally appear in the web page. The exception is the title. The wording here will be visible in the title bar of the web browser. The tag <body> advises that everything that appears between this and its complement, </body>, is the content of the web page and is to be displayed by the web browser.

There are a couple of tags already seen (discussed when talking about website promotion):

```
<! ... >
```

This denotes a comment. Anything within the brackets and preceded by the exclamation mark is a comment made by the writer of the HTML code for their reference or to give information to anyone else who might read the HTML file. These commands are disregarded when the HTML is read by a web browser. Comments can be placed anywhere in a document.

```
<meta ... >
```

Used to define meta data that is (usually) used by search engines and can be populated to give a description of the website or keywords relating to it. Meta data is placed in the head section of the HTML.

Another useful tag is that for a hyperlink. For example, to hyperlink to another site. We might want to say

This site has some great examples of HTML

Clicking on 'This Site' will take you to a different site. The HTML for this would be:

```
<A HREF="http://www.name of website.com/">This
Site</A> has some great examples of HTML
```

Using headings

Now you can start compiling your page itself. HTML lets you define a series of hierarchical headers so that you can provide a page heading, a subheading and a sub-subheading (and so forth). Here's the HTML and the corresponding appearance of the text in the web page:

`<h1>Heading 1</h1>`

Heading 1

`<h2>Heading 2</h2>`

Heading 2

`<h3>Heading 3</h3>`

Heading 3

`<h4>Heading 4</h4>`

Heading 4

`<h5>Heading 5</h5>`

Heading 5

Figure 14.1 Headings – HTML allows multiple levels of headings

You might ask, why do you need headings defined in this way when you could achieve the same by merely specifying different font sizes using the <font size> command? That, of course, would let you specify any font size. The reason that headings are used is that some search engines use them to identify the important text (i.e. the headings!). It also makes it easier if, subsequently, you revise your website. You can change a class of heading throughout your website. Using the <font size> tag you will need to change every occurrence.

Using stylesheets

Publishers of books, magazines and newspapers use stylesheets to define the way their publications look. They will specify the font and font size of the headings, what kind of subheadings are used and the style of, say, bullet points and paragraphs. All contributors to the publication are then told to adhere to the stylesheet in order for there to be a consistent style throughout the publication.

Stylesheets can also be used for websites where the stylesheet defines – as the heading tags did for headings – a consistent approach to the font, font sizes and other parameters throughout a web page and a website. With a stylesheet in place, the HTML writer does not have to specify these parameters for each section of the HTML page. This not only saves a great deal of coding time, it also avoids errors in that the coder does not need to remember to get the tags correct for every change of appearance of the text.

Cascading stylesheets (CSS), as they are known, are increasingly popular for website design. When you use a CSS you can separate the content and the presentational aspects of the web page. You enter the content of the web page in a standard HTML format but then link this page to a CSS which contains the rule base with regard to the layout and display.

The CSS can define virtually all elements of a web page including the placement of images, tables and the use of backgrounds as well as the more mundane text formatting. The result is a much more consistent web page and, consequently, a website that is not only consistent but which can be updated and modified much more easily than using conventional methods.

A stylesheet can be placed directly in the header of an HTML file but it is more usual to create a separate file (identified by the .css suffix). If embedded in a specific HTML file it will also need to be added to other HTML files that may comprise the website. When the CSS file is linked to a group of HTML files it will apply its formatting consistently across all the files.

A call or link to a stylesheet may take a form like this:

```
<link rel="stylesheet" href="http://
www.yoursitename.com/foldername/styles-
site.css" type="text/css" />
```

The example in Figure 14.2 illustrates how a page might look in terms of the 'raw' HTML and how it appears subsequently, after a CSS stylesheet has been applied.

There are other benefits to CSS too. One is that your visitor's browser needs to download less data for each page. That means pages can load faster. It also means that, if you are paying for a fixed amount of bandwidth, you can accommodate far more visitors within your allotted space.

Original HTML page	With stylesheet applied
# Heading 1	# **Heading 1**
## Heading 2	## **Heading 2**
Bold Body Text	**Bold Body Text**
Standard Body Text	Standard Body Text
Alternative Body Text	**Alternative Body Text**

Figure 14.2 Cascading stylesheets make it easy to apply a standard styling across a number of pages

Automated CSS creation

Creating stylesheets can be complex, but some web authoring applications provide basic CSS sheets that you can either use as is, or can apply simple modifications to.

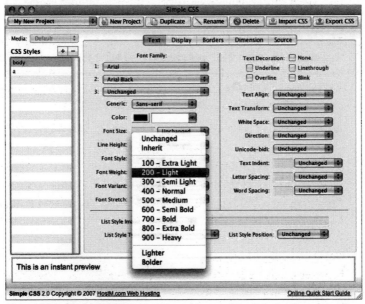

Figure 14.3 Simple CSS – you can create cascading stylesheets very easily using this free application

You will hopefully be pleased to hear that there are even simpler solutions. Free applications like Simple CSS (**www.hostm.com/ css**) let you create CSS very simply indeed. The interface features a wide range of parameters that you can adjust, most by simply making a selection from a drop-down menu.

Summary

As languages go, HTML is straightforward, forgiving and, in web design, a powerful ally to have. You don't need to know it, but if you've been bitten by the bug and want to create a website that's exceptional rather than just great, the knowledge will serve you well. You can experiment using very simple HTML commands – sufficient just to write a line of text – and gradually build both your HTML site and your skills.

Once you've mastered HTML – and it'll take surprisingly little time – you can begin exploring Javascript, XML, ... and all the other web technologies! There are Teach Yourself books for many of these. Look out for:

* **Teach Yourself JavaScript** by Mac Bride

* **Teach Yourself PHP with MySQL** by Nat McBride

15 tips for better websites

In this chapter you will learn:

- some tips for improving your website design and site content
- tips for site management and creating a web store
- about an increasingly important trend in website design

In this final chapter, I thought it would be useful to review some tips and trends relevant to website creation.

Okay, so the tips here are not new but are a summary of the key tips you may have gleaned throughout the book. It's useful to gather them all together so that you can be mindful of them as you create your websites, wikis and blogs. Following on from the tips, I close the book by looking at an increasingly important trend in Web browsing: using mobile devices. I'll take a brief look at how you can make your website 'future safe' by accommodating them.

Website design tips

- Think of visitors when you design your site. Make it easy for them to explore and discover what your site has to offer.

- Make your home page compelling. This is the first stop for most visitors, so let them get the information they want straight away. If that means that they go away (because the site isn't what they expected) don't worry. It's better to have happy surfers than to try to mislead others into lingering.

- Follow an obvious regime for the layout of your site so that visitors can find information easily. Allow them to get to key pages of information in as few clicks as possible.

- Don't bother with flashy (or Flashy) animations preceding the home page. Most visitors will hit the skip button. If you don't have a skip button, visitors could get restless and move on to a different site.

- Go for clear navigation. Visitors will want to navigate your site easily and simply. If they need to spend some time discovering how to move on to the next page, and then find that subsequent navigations are equally counter-intuitive, they may simply give up.

- Keep your site simple. Because you've discovered how to do 101 clever things with your site doesn't mean that you need to use them.

- Avoid garish flashing and luminous text. You want visitors to stay with you and read the content of your page. Don't turn them away with over-bright, flashing text or too many animated elements. Visitors have come to read or view your content not to see how many effects you can pack onto a page.

- Pay attention to the design rules for coloured text and coloured background. Don't sacrifice readability for gimmickry.

- Check your site design in different browsers. If your site doesn't work in a particular browser that could reduce your appeal to visitors. For example, if you've a product that appeals to Mac users, and your site doesn't display properly in Safari, you risk losing a crucial part of your potential market.

- Avoid pop-ups. I've made scant mention of these in this book. Why? Because visitors hate them. They hate them to the point where browsers now let you switch them off. These little windows have become too closely associated with advertising – and slightly iffy advertising at that. Don't use them unless you want to offend your visitors.

Content tips

- It's your site but it's written with visitors in mind. Think about what they would want to see and hear. Keep self-promotion subtle by showing visitors what the site offers them.

- Keep your content fresh. If there's nothing new on your site visitors will stop returning. That doesn't mean you have to discard anything, just make sure that there is new content – particularly on the home page – to ensure visitors that like your site return for more.

- Focus on your visitors. It's easy to try to appeal to everyone rather than your specific market. In doing this you are unlikely to find more visitors and could well alienate those your site was designed for. Enthusiasts and specialists want content that relates to them.

- Be concise. It's easy to pad out your text with superfluous material. Visitors to websites, more than those who read newspapers, books or magazines, don't have the patience to read waffle. They want to extract key facts fast.

♦ Grammar and spelling matter. It should go without saying that all the text on your site needs to be of the highest possible standard. Spelling mistakes are inexcusable, but you'll need to pay attention to grammar too. It takes only a few errors to disenchant a visitor: they are visiting because they consider you a source of knowledge. Spelling and grammar errors will suggest that your content may be below par too.

♦ Don't distract visitors. Don't blast your visitors with text, video and music that all appear simultaneously. Each of the elements may well be compelling when viewed alone but presenting them together will send visitors into sensory overload and have them reaching for the 'Stop' button.

♦ Limit your text to two screenfuls at the maximum. Only articles – which by their nature are a predetermined length – should be longer. For longer articles, make navigation easier by offering hyperlinks back to the top of the page or directly to specific sections.

♦ Keep lines of text down to around 600 pixels wide, or less. Wide text – taking advantage of today's widescreen displays – can be difficult to follow.

♦ Consider accessibility with everything you do with the design and the content.

♦ Use capitalization sparingly. Capitalization draws attention to important words or phrases but use it too often and it loses all impact.

♦ Don't use underline for emphasis. People expect underlined words to be hyperlinks and will try to click on them. When they don't go anywhere they'll get annoyed! Reserve underlining for links and, if you can, follow the convention of colouring the link words blue.

Site management tips

* Keep checking your site visibility with search engines. If, after a reasonable amount of time, it's still invisible (or hard to find) look at revising your search engine optimization.

* Be mindful of the meta tag words too. Use the words that your visitors are likely to use as well as the more formal terms.

* Get friends and peers to critique your site. Get them to visit, explore and comment on the content and functionality. Tell them not to hold back on the comments. You need to understand the visitors' perspective.

* Test your links regularly. You may not have thought that you've changed anything relevant to a particular link when maintaining your site but there's always a chance that you've unintentionally broken a link.

* Where you link to other sites make sure that you test these regularly too. Sites can change their names, disappear or otherwise render the link you've provided redundant.

Web store and shop tips

* Describe your products. Not everyone who visits your store will necessarily know details of what you are selling. Don't put them off by not describing your product for them.

* Illustrate your products. Some people may not know an exact name but will be able to pick the product out from a photo, so make sure you include illustrations. For those that do know the names, it makes it quicker to search and confirms their selection when they can see a photo of it too.

* Make your shop searchable. Unless you have just a few items, you must make it searchable so products can be found easily.

* Make your search facility effective. Make sure the search routine you use can handle misspellings of words and provide close matches as well as exact ones. Some shoppers may spell it 'disk drive' or 'discdrive' rather than 'disc drive' and will be presented with the message 'no results found'. This is shooting yourself in the foot!

◆ Display search results in terms of popularity. Show customers the most popular item first. Many shoppers feel reassured to be buying the same thing as their peers. Unless a shopper asks for a display in this format, avoid listing search matches in order of price. Most expensive first could frighten visitors away, cheapest first will point them towards the cheapest products.

Trends to watch

Mobile web browsing

Mobile phones have had the ability to browse websites for some time. However, for many years this ability was restricted to accessing a small cohort of sites that offered condensed information specially designed for use on the (then) tiny screens of a mobile phone.

The outlook for mobile web browsing got a little brighter with PDAs – personal digital assistants – which offered larger screens, colour, higher resolution and the opportunity to browse just about all of the Web. However the process was still a little clunky and lacked the ease of use that characterizes web browsers used on a computer.

The iPhone generation

Now with the advent of the latest generation of devices – and here the Apple iPhone is the clear exemplar – everything has changed. It's now possible to view and surf on a small pocketable device. And people are doing so voraciously. Mobile web surfing has not only increased substantially following the release of the iPhone, but now around two-thirds of all mobile browsing is done using one. Many website owners are now asking their website designers whether their websites will work effectively on the iPhone.

The expectation is that the iPhone will continue to make inroads into the market and that other, competing products will also help expand this marketplace. It makes sense, then, to ensure that your website will work with an iPhone. For that you could use an iPhone, but if you don't have one or want to be more rigorous in your testing, you can use a simulator.

The iPhone simulator

Helpfully, Apple provides a simulator for testing websites on the iPhone. This provides you with a computer-based (Mac or PC) simulator for the iPhone on which you can put your (or, indeed, any) website through its paces. To get your hands on this simulator you'll need to register for a free developer account by visiting the Apple developer connection at **http://developer. apple.com/iphone/program/**. You can then download the Software Developers Kit (SDK) for free.

You'll find the simulator in the folder developer/platforms/ iPhoneSimulator.platform/Developer/Applications/iPhone Simulator.

Figure 15.1 The iPhone simulator will let you test your website to the full for iPhone mobile browsing capabilities. Orientation changes are perfectly mimicked, just like all other phone features

Run this simulator and you'll be able to run through every aspect of the iPhone's Safari web browser and demo your website. If you are concerned that in doing this you are testing compatibility merely for one device, do remember the penetration of the iPhone and that other pretenders to its throne are likely to use similar standards in their devices. And being able to put the 'Compatible with iPhone' logo on your website imparts a certain cachet!

Summary

As you gain confidence and proficiency in your website construction you'll pick up many hints and tips and, hopefully, the listings above have given you a head start. Creating websites can become an all-consuming passion for some, and a powerful means to an end for others. Whatever category you fall into, remember that getting on the Web can be great fun and, when others recognize your efforts, it becomes extremely rewarding indeed. Thank you for reading and, whether you choose to set up a blog, wiki, gallery or other website, I hope I've helped you in those first steps in getting on the Web.

glossary

Where terms have more than one meaning, the ones that are most relevant to the Internet and the Web are described.

ActiveX: A programming interface (see *API*) that allows web browsers to download and execute certain Windows programs. (See also *Plug-in*.)

Address: See *Web address*.

ADSL (Asymmetric Digital Subscriber Line): The standard broadband line where the upload speed (that from the home computer to a server) is slower than the download speed.

Anchor: The start or end point of a hyperlink.

API (Application Programming Interface): A software interface that lets web browsers (or web servers) communicate with other programs.

ARPAnet: The experimental and embryonic network devised in the 1970s that led to the development of the Internet.

Authentication: A process used by web pages to verify the identity of a user or program. Generally used to check on access for secure web pages.

Back button: A button found on all web browsers' toolbars that returns the user to the document or page previously viewed. A corresponding Forward button goes to the next document/page (this is only active after the Back button has been selected one or more times).

Bandwidth: A measure of the amount of data that can be sent through an Internet connection. The greater the bandwidth, the faster web pages download.

Banner ad: An advertisement placed on a web page (often across the top of a page), that is usually hyperlinked to the advertiser's website.

BBS (Bulletin Board System): A web-based system for sharing ('posting') discussions, documents, files, and announcements. A predecessor of the Forums common in many websites today.

Blog or **weblog:** A type of web page that operates as a public diary for an individual or group. Many blogs can provide *RSS feeds* (q.v.) to allow visitors to subscribe and receive updates as they become available.

Bookmark/Favorite: A stored URL of a web page that enables the user to return quickly to that page.

Browse: The process of following links on a web page. A more casual approach to exploring topics than the more specific process of using a *search engine* (q.v.) to locate information.

Browser or **web browser:** A software program that enables you to view web-formatted documents. It can convert the instructions in web page files into the text, images, sounds, and other features you see. Internet Explorer, Safari and Firefox are popular browsers on both Windows PCs and Macintosh computers.

Cache: An allocated amount of computer memory used by the browser to store web pages, allowing visitors to return quickly to them (using the Forward and Back buttons) without needing to download them again from their original server locations.

CGI (Common Gateway Interface): A way – generally the most common – web programs interact dynamically with users.

Click-through rate: The number of times visitors click on a hyperlink on a page. Advertisers would be keen to know this rate to establish the effectiveness of the page advertising.

Compression: The process of reducing the size of parts of a web page (such as an image) to make downloading faster.

Cookie: An identifier stored on a computer by a web server. It contains information about the user that, when s/he returns to the web page, customizes the page and provides information relevant to the user. Some users block cookies to enhance their security and privacy.

Crawler, web crawler: See *Spider*.

CSS (Cascading Style Sheets): A standardized web coding system that defines a consistent style (such as font, size, colour, spacing, etc.) for web documents.

DHTML (Dynamic HTML): A variation of HTML that defines content that can change dynamically.

Dial-up connection: A connection to Internet via telephone and modem. Unlike broadband (which is typically permanent) dial-up connections are made when required and closed afterwards.

Discussion group: See *Newsgroup*.

Domain name: The initial part of a URL that sits between the http:// (or http://www.) and the first '/' and which identifies the site. It will typically include the name of the organisation, perhaps in an abbreviated form, e.g. microsoft.com, or bbc.co.uk.

Domain name country codes: A scheme of suffixes applied to the URL of a website that can describe its geographical location or its type. Includes .com and .co.uk (general purpose), .edu, .gov, .gov.uk for education and government respectively. Some national codes (such as .tv, for Tuvalu) have been sold outside their geographical location because they produce good website names.

Download: The delivery of data (a web page, document, image) from its original location on the Web to the local computer.

E-mail: Electronic mail. Messages (with or without documents attached) sent from one person to another via the Internet.

E-mail address: The unique address used for sending e-mails. These typically take the format of username@hostname.

E-mail server: A web server designed for and dedicated to the task of serving e-mail.

Favorite: See *Bookmark/Favorite*.

Find tool: A tool found in most browsers that lets a user search for words or phrases on the web page. Similar to the Find tool found in word processors.

Firefox: A freely available browser that is second in popularity to Internet Explorer and suitable for Windows and Macintosh computers. Versions are also compatible with computers that run the Linux and UNIX operating systems.

Flash: A multimedia format based on vector graphics, developed by Macromedia and now owned by Adobe, for use on the web. It was previously called Shockwave Flash and can be used to manipulate vector graphics. (See also *vector graphics*.)

Forward button: See *Back button*.

Frames: A layout for web pages where the page is divided into segments, each of which has its own scroll bars (if the segment is larger than can be displayed in the space allocated in the window) and behaving as separate windows. You can adjust frame dimensions by dragging the frame borders to the requisite size.

FTP (File Transfer Protocol): A network protocol (set of rules) that govern the transfer of data from one computer to another usually, but not exclusively, over the Internet.

FTP server: A web server you can log on to from your computer and download files from, or upload files to.

Gateway: (1) A link between computer programs for sharing data between otherwise incompatible applications or networks. (2) A web page that is designed to attract visitors (and search engines) for the host website.

GIF (Graphics Interchange Format): An image format used extensively on the Web, originating from Compuserve in 1987. It uses data compression to enable comparatively large images to be sent across the Web as much smaller files. The PNG format was developed to replace GIF when there were patent issues with the latter. As those patents have now long expired, both formats are in common usage.

Groups: Discussion forums that are open to any registered contributors where ideas can be shared and questions posed within an online community. Examples are Yahoo Groups and Google Groups. To a certain extent, blogs are replacing some groups.

Head, header (HTML): The top section of the HTML code of web pages. The code begins with <head> and ends with </head>.

It contains the title and description of the page, and a keywords field. The title is what appears in the title bar of the web browser. To view this code, select View Page Source in the browser. This information is also used by some browsers when searching.

Helper application: A program that can enable a browser to display files that it cannot handle itself. (See also *Plug-in*.)

History, search history: A record of all the websites and pages visited when using that browser. This makes it easy to revisit any of those sites by locating the page reference in the History list. The length of the History can often be varied and it can be cleared, if required for security.

Hit count: The number of times a web page (or a discrete part of that page) has been viewed or downloaded.

Host: A computer (normally at a remote location) that delivers web pages to clients or users.

Host name, Hostname: A unique name for a computer or other device attached to a network and the Internet.

Hosting: See *Web hosting*.

HTML (Hypertext Markup Language): The standardized language of computer code that describes web pages and documents, and which contains the text, images and other media along with any links to other documents. HTML also contains formatting instructions for the display of the page on the screen. The HTML code for a page may often include other programming languages such as SGML, XML, Javascript and CGI-script.

HTML document: A document written in HTML.

HTML editor: A software application for editing HTML code. Some word processors can be used for HTML editing but a dedicated HTML editor offers enhanced functionality such as displaying the page as it will be displayed on the Web.

HTTP (Hyper Text Transfer Protocol): A standard set of rules for sending text files across the Internet.

HTTP client: A computer program that requests a service from a web server.

HTTP server: A computer program providing services from a web server.

HTTPS (Hyper Text Transfer Protocol Secure): A secure form of HTTP used in applications such as banking where a secure link between a computer and server needs to be established.

Hypertext: A feature of HTML that allows a word, section of text, image, or other object to become a link to another page, element of a web page or location on the original page. Hypertext linked words are usually (through a convention) coloured blue and underlined to make them more obvious. Clicking on such a word (or other defined area) will take you to the location that the web page designer has determined for that link.

Internet: The collection of interconnected networks and computers that evolved from the ARPAnet project of the late 1960s and early 1970s.

Internet Explorer: The most commonly used web browser, largely because it is bundled with the Windows operating systems. Though claiming a 95% share of the market at its peak around 2002 and 2003, it has been declining since then largely because of interest in the Firefox browser.

Intranet: A private computer network generally used within a company or corporate environment that acts in a similar way to the Internet. Intranets can also allow connection (across the Internet) for home or remote workers.

IP (Internet Protocol) **Address** or **IP Number:** A unique number comprising four blocks of digits separated by full stops. A typical IP address might be: 176.112.216.11. Every computer and device connected to the Internet has its own IP address which enables other devices to identify and contact it.

ISDN (Integrated Services Digital Network): A telephone/telecommunication standard that uses conventional telephone lines to transmit digital data.

ISP (Internet Service Provider): A company that provides Internet access to customers. It may also provide e-mail accounts.

Java: A programming language originally developed by Sun Microsystems to produce compact programs that could be downloaded to a computer (or mobile device) via the Internet. The small Java programs (called *applets*) are free of viruses and other 'malware' that might affect other programs. They are used to provide such features as mini games, animations and clocks. Java is platform-independent, meaning that it can be used on any type of computer and other devices such as PDAs – personal digital assistants – and mobile phones.

Javascript: A simpler programming language than Java (to which it is not related) designed to enable greater interactivity in web pages and to be accessible to those users less skilled in programming than those who use Java.

Keywords: Words searched for using a search command. Useful for finding particular words in an extensive document or web page.

LAN (Local Area Network): A computer network that covers a small area, such as an office, home or school. Computers and other devices may be directly connected to the network by wire, or may connect wirelessly though a wireless hub.

Meta search: A process that searches the metadata linked to a document.

Meta tags: Descriptive tag words added to the HTML of a web page to describe its contents. This forms the basis of any searches carried out by visitors seeking specific information.

Metadata: An item of data that is used to describe other data. An example might be the case of data documents. Those documents are represented by digital data. The metadata would be the data that described those documents – such as the location of the document, the author and a description of the content.

Mosaic: The first commonly available web browser, released in 1993, and now of historical interest only.

Mozilla Foundation: A non-profit organization set up to support the open source Mozilla project. It has developed a number of web browsers, the most popular of which is Firefox.

Newsgroup: A discussion group operated through, and across, the Internet.

Packet: A small, discrete block of data. When data is sent over the Internet, it travels in small formatted blocks, rather than a continuous stream. This makes it simpler to recover from interruptions in the connections.

Page hits: See *Hit count*.

PDF (Portable Document Format): A file format developed by Adobe Systems, used to exchange documents, irrespective of the host and destination computers. Virtually any document, text, image or a combination, can be converted to PDF format. To be read, the receiving computer needs a PDF reader such as the free Adobe Reader software. Apart from platform independence, an advantage of the PDF format is that it is difficult for a recipient to alter the file, making it a more effective way of sharing information securely.

Personal page: A web page created by an individual, rather than one created by, or on behalf of, a corporation, institution or other organization. The page often links to other pages on the site or on different sites that reflect subjects and issues important to the individual.

Phrase: A group of keywords used in a search. Normally, quotation marks are used to define the phrase, in which case the search tools will look for the occurrence of the whole phrase rather than the individual words.

Plug-in: A small program or application built into (or added to) a web browser to extend the functionality. Plug-ins are used to play certain video files or view specific document types.

PNG (Portable Network Graphics): An image format used on the web. (See also *GIF*.)

Raster graphics: See *Vector graphics*.

Redirection: When a visitor to a web page types in its address, that page may automatically forward to another site. This may be because the owner of a site wants to use a more memorable address than that of the actual site. For example, the website **www.petercope.co.uk** may redirect the user to the rather less memorable **www.users.seymournet.com/112705/users/pcope**.

RSS or RSS feeds: Short for 'Really Simple Syndication', a subscription service offered by some websites that delivers a summary of new content.

Safari: Web browser included in the Macintosh OS X operating system and used in the Apple iPhone and iPod Touch. Also available in a Windows-compatible version.

Search engine: A computer program used to search, catalogue and rank the billions of pages on the Web and provide listings in response to user requests. Google is the most commonly used general purpose search engine.

Search results, popularity ranking of: A method used by some search engines where results of a search are displayed according to the popularity of the sites. Popularity uses an inexact principle that measures how many other sites link to each page. This assumes that many links implies popularity, which may or may not be true. Google generally searches in this manner.

Search results, relevancy ranking of: Results that are displayed in order of their relevance to the search term. Search engines use a technique called fuzzy logic to help the search tools find those sites that are increasingly less relevant to the precise search term and order them accordingly.

Server, web server: A computer with an extensive array of hard disks optimized for running websites, connected to the Internet and delivering web pages to remote computers when requested. Most web servers have security systems and backup regimes that ensure that, should a disk fail, the data on it can be accessed from a copy elsewhere on that server or on an alternative one, ensuring continuity of any websites. Web servers are usually hosted by large organizations and ISPs, but it is possible (though rarely recommended) to use a domestic computer as such.

SHTML: A computer file extension (or suffix) usually shown as .shtml to indicate a file that uses a scripting language called Server Side Includes (SSI). These files are used to include the contents of a file in another file that is being delivered by a web server.

Site, web site, website: A collection of web pages hosted on one (or, for security, more than one) web server.

Spiders, web spiders: Also known as web crawlers, web robots, these are computer programs that continuously browse the World Wide Web in a systematic manner looking for new data and information. This is passed to search engines to assist them in their searches of the Web and ensure that the results returned are the most up to date possible.

Streaming: A technique for sending audio and video files over the Internet so that it can be listened to or viewed ahead of the file being fully downloaded.

Streaming format: A file format used for streaming content across the Internet. Most popular are QuickTime, Windows Media and Real Video.

SVG (Scalable Vector Graphics): SVG is both an XML specification and a file format for describing vector graphics (q.v.) that can be still graphics or animated.

TCP/IP (Transmission Control Protocol/Internet Protocol): The collection of protocols or instructions that fundamentally defines the Internet. These were originally designed for the UNIX operating system but appropriate TCP/IP software is now available for all computer operating systems.

TELNET: A contraction of Telecommunications Network, this is a largely superseded technique that allows a computer to log onto another via the Internet.

Title: Contained in the metadata, the 'official' title of a document that will appear in the top bar of the browser window when the document is displayed. It will also be listed in the results returned by a search engine.

URL (Uniform Resource Locator): A unique address of any Web document. The URL is what you type into a web browser when you want it to navigate to the associated page.

Vector graphics: A method of creating graphics that uses mathematical equations to define its components. This has the benefit of allowing the design to be scaled up or down without affecting the integrity of the graphic. The alternative raster graphics are based on pixels in the same way as digital images. When raster graphics are scaled up the pixel nature becomes obvious because the resolution is fixed.

W3C (World Wide Web Consortium): The organization with overall responsibility for managing standards used on the World Wide Web.

WAN (wide area network): A computer network that covers a broad area (compared to a local area network, that covers a more concise area) that may include several cities and cross national boundaries. This may be hard wired (in that the network is 'closed', and all computers are connected directly to this network) or it may use public connections to establish all the links. Generally used to link the offices or sites of large corporations.

Web address: Alternative common name for a Uniform Resource Locator (URL).

Web browser: See *Browser*.

Web hosting, web hosting service: A service that provides disk space on a web server for clients' websites and Internet activity for visitors to that website. Web hosting services generally take responsibility for ensuring that the data comprising websites entrusted to it are backed up and copied so that it is protected in the case of a system failure.

Web server: See *Server*.

Wiki: Deriving its name from the Hawaiian for 'quick', a wiki is a collection of web pages that are focused on a project and usually collaborative in nature. Such pages are usually updated and contributed to by a group of people rather than one individual. The best known wiki is the encyclopaedia, Wikipedia.

Wireless hub, wireless Internet router: A gateway through which computers and other devices (PDAs, games consoles) can connect wirelessly to the Internet. Most hubs also provide for a wired connection and many provide a connection for a printer so that a printer can be shared by all the computers that connect via the hub.

WWW, World Wide Web: The global network of computers that use the Internet to exchange web pages and information.

XHTML (Extensible HTML): A hybrid between HTML and XML that does not suffer the compatibility issues that XML does with regard to its use in web pages and search engines.

XML (Extensible Markup Language): A web page programming language that is commonly used for pages emerging from databases and other applications where parts of the page are repeatedly displayed in a standard format. It is called Extensible because users can define their own elements within it and this can sometimes lead to compatibility problems.